THE LIBRARY
ST. MARY'S COLLEGE OF MARYLAND
ST MARY'S CITY, MARYLAND 20686

EARLY
NEW ENGLAND
PSALMODY

Da Capo Press Music Reprint Series

GENERAL EDITOR

FREDERICK FREEDMAN

VASSAR COLLEGE

EARLY
NEW ENGLAND
PSALMODY

AN HISTORICAL APPRECIATION
1620–1820

By HAMILTON C. MACDOUGALL

𝄞 DA CAPO PRESS • NEW YORK • 1969

A Da Capo Press Reprint Edition

This Da Capo Press edition of Hamilton C. Macdougall's *Early New England Psalmody* is an unabridged republication of the first edition published in Brattleboro, Vermont, in 1940 by Stephen Daye Press.

Library of Congress Catalog Card Number 79-87398

Published by Da Capo Press
A Division of Plenum Publishing Corporation
227 West 17th Street
New York, N. Y. 10011

All rights reserved

Printed in the United States of America

1-26-79

EARLY
NEW ENGLAND
PSALMODY

AN HISTORICAL APPRECIATION
1620–1820

By HAMILTON C. MACDOUGALL

Doctor of Music, Brown University
Associate, Royal College of Organists, London
Professor Emeritus of Music, Wellesley College

STEPHEN DAYE PRESS :: BRATTLEBORO

COPYRIGHT, 1940, BY HAMILTON C. MACDOUGALL

PRINTED IN THE UNITED STATES OF AMERICA

TO
CAROLINE HAZARD
IN ACKNOWLEDGMENT
OF HELPFUL SUGGESTIONS
AND UNREMITTING
INTEREST

Preface

What music did the Pilgrims and Puritans of New England use when singing their psalms? What is its history? How did it find the way to Plymouth and Massachusetts Bay? When did the New England singers begin to write their own psalm tunes? Who were these singer-composers? What were their musical standards? What is the value of their music, judged by twentieth century taste? When did it become obsolescent?

In the following discussion of such questions, it will be noted that here is a study of the music itself, the book not concerning itself with biographical, religious, or musicological detail; such latter surveys have had full treatment from various authors.

The Puritan psalmody *per se,* however, has received comparatively little attention. When treated, it has been laughed at, possibly because of the writers' ignorance of its origins and history.[1]

The origin of the early psalm tunes used in New England may be traced to the music of the Protestant Reformation in Germany, France, Scotland, and England; their histories may be interestingly followed in the Genevan, Scottish, and English psalters of the sixteenth century, up to their inclusion in *The Bay Psalm Book* and the works of John Tufts, Thomas Walter and others.

It was William Billings (1770) who was the first New Englander to make his own music and to influence his contemporaries, Andrew Law, Lewis Edson, Jacob French, Oliver Holden, Samuel Holyoke, Joseph Kimball and others. Billings's influence was great; he vitalized the music of his group for a full thirty years. Particularly with his 'fuguing tunes' did Billings capture the enthusiastic imitation of the music-writers of the day who agreed with him in his admiration of the fugue form.

Owing to various causes, (a) revolt against the Billings technique

---

[1] For a more direct account of these disparagements of New England's early psalmody consult Dr. Percy A. Scholes's valuable work, *The Puritans and Music,* Oxford University Press, London, 1934, pp. xxii-428, in which (pp. 7-12) Dr. Scholes quotes twenty-eight authors who belittle the psalm tunes and the psalm-singing of the Puritans.

and ideology beginning as early as 1795, (b) the immigration of excellent musicians from Europe, and (c) political changes in the United States growing out of the Revolution of '76, the war of 1812 and the birth of a national consciousness, it is logical to date the death of the old New England music-period and the birth of a new era as around 1820.

The list of chapter headings herein will show the expansion of these few leading ideas into their complete exposition. A few related or ancillary topics (the singing school, the New England singing teacher and his problems, the 'grounds' of music, experiments in musical notation) are expanded into chapters; these are germane to the purpose of the book, which is to treat intensively and appreciatively of New England sacred music, from 1620 to 1820.

Since this to my knowledge has never been done, the book is offered as a contribution to a critical and methodical treatment of the subject.

It will be discovered by the reader that there are fields for re search open to those who are interested in our musical history.

It remains to make my acknowledgements to those individuals and libraries whose help has made this work possible. I hereby record my sincere thanks to Mr. James T. Lightwood and Dr. Percy A. Scholes, who have read the manuscript and made most helpful (sometimes painful) criticisms, from which I hope I have profited; to the staffs of the Boston Public Library (Allen A. Brown special collection) and Boston University (library of the Theological School); library of the Essex Institute (Salem); to the library of the Massachusetts Historical Society (Boston); to the Hartford Foundation, Mr. Charles B. Thayer, librarian; particularly to the special Lowell Mason library (at the Library of the School of Music, Yale University), Miss O'Meara, librarian; to Professor Mary T. Noss (Ohio University), who has been of much assistance in translations from the French; and to my wife for her never-failing coöperation and warm sympathy.

HAMILTON C. MACDOUGALL.

Wellesley, Massachusetts
May, 1939

Table of Contents

Illustrations

CHAPTER ONE

Music of The Protestant Reformation in Bohemia and Germany

To music the Protestant Reformation owed more than we are perhaps accustomed to realize. The metrical versions of the Psalms in France with their associated melodies, the hymns and chorals of Germany, the Psalms and psalm tunes in England, all these using the people's language rather than the Latin of the church, were sources of great strength in the religious movements linked with the names of John Huss (ca. 1373-1415), Martin Luther (1483-1548), John Calvin (1509-1564), and the English reformers. The poets, Clément Marot, Théodore de Bèze in France, Martin Luther in Germany, Sternhold and Hopkins, Tate and Brady, William Kethe in England, with Wedderburn, Robert Pont and John Craig in Scotland, bore the brunt of the labor of paraphrasing or of translating the Psalms into the vernacular.

Huss or Hus, John, reformer and martyr, son of a Bohemian peasant, propagated the reform doctrines of the Englishman Wycliffe and so came under the condemnation of his ecclesiastical superiors. Huss was tried for heresy, was condemned and in 1415 burnt at the stake. It was he who realized that there are other ways of reaching the hearts of the people than through sermons and treatises.[1]

---

[1] Huss's followers, the Bohemian Brethren, used a tune (*Ave Hierarchia* or *Ravenshaw*) probably an adaptation from the mediaeval German melody of the sixteenth century. Under the title "Gottes Sohn ist kommen" it appears in the *Evangelical Lutheran Hymnal*, Concordia Publishing House, St. Louis, 1931, complete in a six-line form; *Hymns Ancient and Modern* shortens it to four-lines. It is generally included in the shorter form in most of the hymnals, American and English. The Hussite movement was in the fourteenth century, before the days of the printing press; consequently the output was small for the dissemination of hymns compared with what was feasible at the Reformation. See *Hymns Ancient and Modern*, historical edition, xxxvii and 397, Wm. Clowes and Son, Ltd., London, 1909.

Martin Luther was born at Eisleben, Germany: his father, a miner; his mother, a woman of exemplary virtue. Luther was ordained a priest and removed to Wittenberg, becoming a teacher in the university there. It was on the door of the church in Wittenberg (1517) that he nailed his ninety-five theses against indulgences. In 1530 the Ausburg Confession, an expression of the culmination of the German Reformation, was drawn up. Luther was one of the great leaders of sacred song, his hymns being intense, expressive, and of enduring power. Lightwood remarks[2] that "Luther fully realized the good done by the followers of Huss; but as their hymns were first published in a language foreign to the Germans, he was unable to use them." Writing to a friend, Luther says, "We Germans lack poets and musicians, or they are unknown to us, who are able to make Christian and spiritual songs of such value that they can be used daily in the house of the Lord." Luther therefore resolved to devote his poetical and musical talents to the service of God. He wrote thirty-seven hymns, twenty-one of them in 1523. His authorship of the tunes often attributed to him has been disputed.[3]

When one considers how great the debt of twentieth century English and American hymnals to Luther and the German chorale it is surprising to learn that in the early days of the sixteenth century the Lutheran hymnody had very little influence in England.[4] In the days of Henry the Eighth there was a brief moment when Lutheranism seemed likely to count for much in English religious

---

[2] *Hymn-tunes and Their Story*, James T. Lightwood, The Epworth Press, London, 1905.

[3] *The English Hymnal*, Oxford University Press, London, 1933, *Hymns Ancient and Modern*, historical edition, 1909, and hymnals in general credit Luther with the melody of "Ein' feste Burg." James Moffat, however, editor of *Handbook to the Church Hymnary*, revised edition, 1927, states: "Tradition has credited Luther with the composition of a number of original chorales. Exact proof of his authorship is lacking; he himself never advances any claim to have composed a single air." "Luther's Hymn" melody is in "Geistliche Lieder," Wittenberg, 1535. For a full and enlightening discussion of the whole matter see *Hymn-tunes and Their Story*, pp. 7-14.

[4] M. S. Lathrop Thorndike (see *Publications of the Colonial Society of Massachusetts*, Vol. I, 228-239) thinks that is easily explained. "It is noteworthy," he writes, "that the Lutheran Reformation in Germany, though often spoken of in connection with the English Reformation which followed it, had little effect upon or sympathy with the later upheaval. The Lutherans were more monarchical in politics and more conservative in creed. They averred that they would rather turn back to Rome than tolerate heretics who denied the corporal presence."

reform, but it soon lapsed, leaving no mark at all on the hymnody of the English church. There is one book which sums up history so far as this latter point is concerned, *Goostly Psalmes and Spiritualle Songes* of Miles Coverdale (1488-1568), published about 1539; it represented an attempt to import Lutheran hymnody into England. But the book was included in the list of prohibited books.[5] It was over two hundred years after the publication of Calvin's *Genevan Psalter* (1562) before Jacobi published the *Psalmodia Germanica* (1772). Later hymnals pay belated homage to the hymns and tunes of Luther's day and those of the century following.[6]

---

[5] See *Hymns Ancient and Modern*, 1909, pp. xxxvii-xxxviii, and Livingston's reprint, 1864, of the 1635 *Scottish Metrical Psalter*, p. 9. See also note 18.

[6] A somewhat careful inspection of three of the English hymnals of widest circulation gives the following numbers of tunes of German origin included: *English Hymnal*, 20% of the total number of tunes; *Hymns Ancient and Modern*, Wm. Clowes & Son Ltd., London, 1924, 15%; and *The Methodist Hymn-book*, Methodist Conference Office, London, 1933, 7%.

CHAPTER TWO

Music of The Protestant Reformation in France

The Protestant Reformation in France centers about the somewhat dour personality of John Calvin, who became interested in the reform doctrines early in life, resigned the preferment he held in the Church, and after several years of wandering settled down in Geneva in 1541. Calvin did a great deal for psalmody although he was in no sense a music-lover and had not as keen a realization of the value of music in worship and devotion as had Martin Luther. Calvin's period of greatest activity in his Genevan Church extended from 1541 to 1561.[7] He reduced the whole substance of worship to praying, preaching and singing. He projected a species of religious song consisting of the Psalms as a whole translated into the vernacular (that is into French) and adapted to plain and easy melodies which could be sung not only in the churches but used in every walk and condition in life. Thus did Calvin plan the great work that afterward became the *Genevan Psalter*, completed in 1562.[8]

It was the French poet, Clément Marot (1497-1544) who contributed largely to the *Genevan Psalter*. Sir Richard R. Terry writes, "History is full of strange ironies, but none more strange than the change of circumstances which led to metrical psalmody

---

[7] "Very different estimates have been formed of Calvin's character. Stern in spirit and unyielding in will, he is never petty or selfish in his motives. Nowhere amiable, he is everywhere strong. Arbitrary and cruel he is yet heroic in his aims, and beneficent in the scope of his ambition. His moral purpose is always clear and definite —to live a life of duty, to shape circumstances to such divine ends as he apprehended, and to work out as he understood it, the glory of God." (*Funk and Wagnall's Standard Encyclopedia*, article, "Calvin.") In this connection pp. 332-344 in Dr. Percy A. Scholes's *The Puritans and Music*, Oxford University Press, London, 1934 should be read.

[8] See *The Music of the French Psalter*, Waldo Selden Pratt, Columbia University Press, New York, 1939.

beginning as the favorite of a gay Catholic court and ending as the exclusive hall-mark of the severest form of Protestantism. Marot and not Calvin was the *fons et origo* of metrical psalmody. The Psalms of David formed an integral part of Christian worship from the very beginning; in Western Europe they were sung in Latin. It was in Marot's time that the translation of the Psalms into vernacular verse was attempted on an intensive scale. His thirty Psalms, published in 1536-1539 without attached melodies, leaped for various reasons into popularity and were sung by Catholics and Protestants alike, and to popular airs of the day. Twelve of these appeared in the Calvin *Strasbourg Psalter* (1539), to Marot's surprise; and at Geneva in accordance with Calvin's request he paraphrased twenty more; in 1543 his *Cinquante Psaumes* and a few other things were included. Marot never mentions Calvin, and Calvin alludes to Marot twice only in letters but never utters a word of thanks for Marot's poetical work. Marot died in August, 1544, and was buried in the Catholic church of St. Jean, Turin."[9]

The startling incongruity between Marot, gay and fashionable man about town, and Marot the poet of Protestantism, does not seriously trouble Jacques Piollen, who writes in *Le Psautier Huguenot, Choix de 54 vieux Psaumes* (1928, ed. by Pierre Devoluy),

"Le procès, longtemps discuté, est, je pense, maintenant jugé: Clément Marot appartient à la Réforme. Non seulement ses rudes attaques contre les 'sorbonistes,' les moines, les abus de l'Eglise, rémoignent de son détachement de la religion romaine, mais aussi, mais surtout, il a vécu, il a souffert à cause de ses œuvres religieuses, qui faisaient plus que 'sentir le fagot,' qui étaient une contribution positive à l'œuvre de réforme entreprise par les esprits les plus sages, les plus sérieux, les plus savants de la France de François I[et].
Et, sans doute, Marot ne fut pas toujours, comme d'autres, sage et sérieux. Ce page de Villeroy, devenu pensionnaire de la duchesse d'Alençon, puis valet de chambre du roi, a toujours aimé la liberté de conduite, et même la liberté des mœurs. Ce poète de cour est resté toujours l'ami des manières mondaines, voire galantes. Sa figure avenante et vive ne rappelle point celle de Théodore de Bèze, empreinte d'une si grave sévérité. Mais tous les huguenots pouvaient-ils ressembler à Calvin ou à Bèze? Et si vous me dites: 'Il n'a pas

[9] *Calvin's First Psalter* (1539), Sir Richard R. Terry, Ernest Benn, Ltd., London, 1932, pp. ii, iii, iv.

l'air protestant,' je vous prierai de ne plus considérer son visage, mais relire ses œuvres, de méditer sur sa vie."

Thomas Warton, in his *History of English Poetry*,[10] is of the opinion that certain aspects of Calvin's theories of worship are open to criticism. (Warton was a stalwart Churchman and admirer of the noble liturgy of the Church of England.)

"Calvin's music was intended to correspond with the general parsimonious spirit of his worship; not to captivate the passions and seduce the mind by a levity, a variety or richness of modulation, but to infuse the more sober and ravishing ecstasies. The music he permitted, although it had sometimes wonderful effects, was to be without grace, elegance, and elevation. These apt notes were about forty tunes of one part only and in unisonous key; remarkable for a certain strain of sombrous gravity and applicable to all the psalms in their turns, as the stanzas and sense might allow. They also appear in the subsequent impressions of 1564 and 1577. They are believed to contain some of the original melodies composed by French and German musicians. Many of them, particularly the celebrated one of the Hundredth Psalm, probably by Bourgeois, are the tunes of Goudimel and LeJeune, who are among the first composers of the music of Marot's French Psalms".[11] (Warton was misinformed here.) "Not a few were probably carried to England by the Protestant manufacturers of cloth in Flanders and the Low Countries, who fled into England from religious persecution and settled in those countries where their art now chiefly flourishes. It is not, however, unlikely that some of our own musicians, who lived about the year 1562, and could always tune their harps to the religion of the times, such as Merbeck, Tallis, Tye, Parson and Munday were employed on this occasion: yet under the restriction of conforming to the jejune and unadorned work of the foreign composers. I presume much of the primitive harmony of those ancient tunes is now lost by additions, variations and transpositions."

---

[10] Edited by W. Carew Hazlitt, London, 1871, vol. iv, *passim*.

[11] A valuable source-book for this period is *Clément Marot et Le Psautier Huguenot* . . . par C. Douen, à L'Imprimerie Nationale, Paris, 1878. Two vols. pp. 1461.

6

CHAPTER THREE

Music of The Protestant Reformation in England

The Reformation in England led, in the reign of Henry VIII (1491-1547), who ascended the throne in 1509, to the abolition of the papal supremacy and the liberation from papal control of the Church of England. Under Edward VI (1537-1553), who succeeded Henry VIII, occurred the introduction of the Book of Common Prayer and the publication of the forty-two Articles of Religion. (In 1562, under Archbishop Parker, fourth year of Elizabeth, this gave place to thirty-nine Articles.) Mary Tudor (1516-1558), succeeding Edward VI, was queen from 1553 to 1558; in 1555 Parliament restored the papal power and revived the laws against heresy. During Mary Tudor's reign life was made very unpleasant for the reformers; how far she was responsible for the cruelties practiced on them is doubtful. There was an exodus to the Continent of many of those who had espoused the Reformation. The Protestant cause, nourished for a time under Edward VI, was for the time definitely lost. The fleeing Protestants found asylum principally in Strasbourg, Frankfort-on-the-Main, Emden, Wesel, Zurich and, later, Geneva. The English Church at Geneva had one hundred and eighty-six members. Between eight hundred and one thousand English and Scotch, including many distinguished persons (John Knox was one), remained on the Continent until the accession of Elizabeth (November, 1558).[12]

As in the early settlements in America, so in 1553-1558 the exiles were divided according to Maxwell (op. cit.) into two classes, Anglican and Calvinist, although all were Protestants. Early in 1559 the exiles began to find their way back to England and Scotland to take their share in the reconstruction awaiting them. With them they carried back to England the psalter now known as the *Anglo-*

---

[12] For a full treatment of this whole period see *John Knox's Genevan Service Book*, Maxwell, Oliver & Boyd, Edinburgh, 1931.

Genevan Psalter, and to Scotland, John Knox's *Form of Prayers*, later to become the *Book of our Common Order* used in Scotland until superseded by the Westminster *Directory* in 1645.[13] Maxwell tells us (op. cit.) that it was as early as 1525 that psalms and hymns began to appear in the Reformers' service books; the metrical psalms and canticles were a popular part of the reformed services, adoration, thanksgiving, praise and prayer were embodied in them. The psalms were the people's part in the worship of the reformed church everywhere . . . . the Reformers did not destroy, but restored to the people their part in worship.[14]

It was in 1539 that Calvin's *First Psalter* appeared. Twenty-three years later, 1562, the complete *Calvin (Genevan) Psalter* was issued; and at the same time the complete *Sternhold & Hopkins Psalter* was given to the English. For one hundred and fifty years this latter psalter was in use by all English-speaking people, and so is usually referred to as the Old Version (O.V.). The 1562 edition contained words and music (melodies only), but by singing several psalms to the same tune it was possible to take care of the one hundred and fifty psalms with forty-six tunes. From the name of the printer this is often referred to as the *Day Psalter*. In 1563 the tunes of the 1562 edition, with many more, were published in vocal-part books for four voices; it was in the seventeen hundreds (in New England) that the work of Sternhold and Hopkins (the 'old' psalter) was ousted by the *Tate & Brady Psalter*, 1696, usually referred to as the 'new' psalter,[15] and also as the New Version (N.V.).

This may be as good a time as any to call attention to the disparity in varieties of meter between the French and English psalters of 1562. Sir R. Terry[16] discloses a great variety in the length of stanzas, in the length of single lines and consequently in the general metric scheme. The 1562 version of Calvin in like manner is rich in metrical construction. In great contrast with all this is the

---

[13] In study of this period Maxwell, and the historical edition of *Hymns Ancient and Modern*, will be found valuable.

[14] The Henry Expert reprint of Calvin's 1562 *Psalter* in French (Paris), having Calvin's own notes, the metrical translations, and the melodies, is extremely useful. See also Appendix L.

[15] *Tate & Brady* was sanctioned by an Order in Council in 1696.

[16] Op. cit.

8

metric scheme of *Sternhold & Hopkins*, which is chiefly Common Meter or 'ballad' meter, i.e., lines of eight and six syllables alternating: 8.6.8.6.8.6.8.6., known as D.C.M. and 8.6.8.6., known as C.M. The C.M. or short stanza was used more freely as time went on, although both D.C.M. and C.M. still find a place in the older metrical psalms.

Warton[17] justifiably waxes bitingly satirical when he describes the style and versification of the *Day Psalter*. The general tenor of his criticism is that of severe artistic condemnation accompanied by a certain condonation of the offenses as due to the times in which Sternhold and Hopkins worked, and differences in standards between the sixteenth and seventeenth centuries. In this connection a quotation or two cannot be resisted: "John Hopkins expostulates with the Deity in these ludicrous, at least trivial expressions:

> 'Why doost withdraw thy hand aback,
> And hide it in thy lappe?
> O plucke it out and be not slack
> To give thy foes a rappe!' "

But Warton gives qualified praise to the following famous lines by Sternhold (used later by the New England composer, William Billings):

> "The Lord descended from above,
> And bowed the heavens high;
> And underneath his feet he cast
> The darkness of the sky.
> On Cherubs and on Seraphims
> Full roiallie he rode:
> And on the winges of all the windes
> Came flying all abrode."

Warton's *History*, vol. iv, pp. 124-139, is well worth reading for his account of the principal actors in the French drama of the Reformation, Marot, Calvin, John Knox, and Guillaume de Franc (who for a long time was credited with having composed the Old Hundredth psalm-tune), though he does not seem to have known about either Goudimel or Bourgeois, who were even more important than de Franc. Warton probably expressed contemporary criticism in his remarks about the 'old' psalter.

---

[17] Op. cit.

9

CHAPTER FOUR

Music of the Protestant Reformation in Scotland

New England psalmody not only inherited from the Genevan and the various English psalters, as I will show specifically later, but also owed something to another psalter, less well known than the *Day Psalter*, but quite as interesting as either of the others named, viz. the *Scottish Psalter*. The complete *Scottish Psalter* was issued in 1564. Syllabic tunes, that is, those having one note and one note only for each syllable of the words, were adopted and captured the liking of the multitude. The difficulty of learning tunes for each of the numerous psalms resulted in what were termed 'common tunes', tunes that might be used for any psalm of the same metre.

Calvin had refused to allow part-singing in Geneva; but in Scotland 'sang-schules' established before the Reformation, continued long after it, helping to furnish a body of educated singers. The 1635 *Scottish Psalter* represents the high-water mark of the Reformation psalmody, proving as it does the existence of great skill among the Scottish people as well as among the musicians. Besides the 'common' tunes there were 'rapports' or 'reports', and finally the 'proper' tunes, that is, those identified in each case with a special psalm; in the 1635 *Scottish Psalter* there were thirty-one 'common', eight 'reports', and one hundred and four 'proper' tunes.[18] 'Reports' may be described as tunes for four voices made up entirely or in part by the voices entering on points of imitation, though seldom in strict fugal style. It has been suggested that the 'report' was the ancestor of the 'fuguing tune' so popular in the

---

[18] These matters are disposed of entertainingly in *Manual of Church Praise*, The Church of Scotland Committee on Publications, Edinburgh, 1932, pp. 32-37; and exhaustively in *The Scottish Metrical Psalter* of A.D., 1635, edited by the Rev. Neil Livingston, Maclure J. Macdonald, Glasgow, 1864.

later New England psalmody. The Rev. Neil Livingston was of that opinion.[19] In the 1635 *Scottish Psalter* a great majority of the tunes were in four parts, melodies always in the tenor. Tunes like *Dundee, Windsor, London New* and *York* are C.M. tunes characteristic of the contributions of the Scottish psalmody to modern American hymnals, via New England psalmody.

In bringing to a close this imperfect summary of the Reformation in Bohemia, Germany, France and Britain as expressed in the hymns, their tunes, and the more important metrical psalters I cannot refrain from quoting the acute differentiation made by Sir Richard Terry between the German and Genevan contributions to reform. He says (op. cit., p. xxii):

> "In view of the intimate relationship, in their early stages, between Lutheran and Calvinistic Psalmody, the later developments of each must always be of interest not only to the historian and the critic, but also to that very large body of private individuals to whom psalmody appeals. . . . Not only were additions made to the Lutheran books, but the tunes themselves, under the treatment of one musician after another, blossomed out—from their original simplicity and dignity—into an infinite variety of form and structure, until in Johann Sebastian Bach their efflorescence took on the luxuriance of a tropical forest wherein succeeding generations might take their pastime. The *Genevan Psalter* on the contrary, reached its artistic zenith during the lifetime of those who compiled it. The *Strasbourg Psalter* of Calvin was published with its melodies unharmonized. Subsequent Huguenot Psalters were, for some years, published without any tunes at all. Then came Bourgeois and Goudimel, the *Genevan Psalter*, with their strong dignified harmonies, which are as fresh today as they were four hundred years ago. But that was the end. There they remain. There was no development of them at the hands of later musicians as in the case of the Lutheran Choral."

The historical edition of *Hymns Ancient and Modern* (1904) gives a full account of the psalters antedating and following the *Day Psalter*. Considerable information about the same period, with particular reference to Scottish psalmody, is in Neil Livingston (op. cit.).

Attention is called to *The Scottish Psalter of 1635*, edited with modal harmonies by Richard Runciman Terry (London, Novello

---

[19] "The Reports seem to have been the forerunner of the fugues, repeats, etc. which in after times became so abundant." *Scottish Metrical Psalter*, 1635.

and Company Limited, January, 1935). The immediate purpose of the book is to bring the old melodies back into practicable, singable form. Part 1, therefore, consists of the tunes reduced to four parts, short score, transposed to convenient pitch for congregational use with the melody in the soprano. Part 2 is a reprint of the Livingston edition of the 1635 *Psalter* now difficult to obtain. Those who, like Terry, are impressed by the high value of the work, *The Scottish Metrical Psalter of 1635* by Livingston, will be glad to read Terry's sympathetic account of Livingston in Terry's own edition, pp. ix-x. Those who wish to pursue the study of the modal characteristics of the *Psalter* tunes ought to look up pp. 44-45 and 54 in the Livingston edition.

CHAPTER FIVE

The Este and Ainsworth Psalters

We have by no means exhausted the list of early English psalters contributing more or less to the seventeenth century New England psalmody; there are still two psalters, those of Este (1592) and Ainsworth (1612) that find their places here.

The *Este Psalter* is accessible through the Rimbault reprint which, while not a literal reprint but rather a bringing of the separate parts into a score, is believed to be trustworthy.[20] There are several things that give interest to the *Este Psalter*. It is probably the first collection of psalm-tunes some of which are named for places; these (see Rimbault reprint) are *London Old* (Psalm 50), *Winchester* (Psalm 84), *Glassenburie* (Psalm 88), *Kentish Tune* (Psalm 92), and *Cheshire Tune* (Psalm 146). We find with surprise that it uses the C clefs as well as the F and G; it retains the air in the tenor; since the fifty-eight tunes in the *Psalter* are harmonized by ten of the best musicians of the day it is a source-book for the study of the harmony of the period. After Este, Ravenscroft was prodigal of place-names for tunes, and their lead was followed by all the composers of the day and by those following up to the present.[21] The C clefs find place today in orchestral scores, but they were dropped from the New England singing-

---

[20] *The Whole Book of Psalms/with the tunes in four Parts,/first published by/ Thomas Este,/A.D. 1592,/edited by/Edward F. Rimbault, LL.D., F.S.A.,/printed for the members/of the/Musical Antiquarian Society./* (n.d.) The original *Este* had the treble on the top of the left hand page, the tenor or air being below it; the altus was at the top of the right hand page, with the bassus below it. Rimbault has barred the music and retained the key signatures; in his preface he maintains his careful accuracy and his abstention from tampering.

[21] In using place names for their tunes the New England compilers and composers thus followed good models. *The Bay Psalm Book*, 22nd edition, 1729, had 11 tunes, 5 place-named; Reverend Mr. Tufts's *Introduction to the Singing of Psalm-Tunes*, 5th edition, 1726, had 37 tunes, 17 place-named; *Urania*, James Lyon, 1761, 66 tunes, 28 place-named; *Village Harmony*, 5th edition, 1800, 242 tunes, 148 place-named, etc.

school collections in the later eighteen-hundreds. The treble took the melody away from the tenor at the same time, with the conservatives remonstrating loudly.

An analysis of the harmony in *Este*[22] shows the musical material of the tunes to consist of the tonic, supertonic, subdominant, dominant and submediant triads in their root position or first inversion; the second inversion seems to have been avoided unless the fourth from its bass was prepared. The ordinary 'authentic cadence' (tonic six-four, dominant, tonic) does not appear. Dominant sevenths occur, but the seventh is prepared and resolved; the inversions of the dominant seventh are not used, and no seventh chords other than the dominant seventh are allowed. An exception must be made of the chord of the 'added sixth', which is really the subdominant triad in root position, with the sixth from the bass note added. (It is not the first inversion of the supertonic seventh, for the seventh is not resolved.) Passing-tones play no great part, but tunes in minor keys are very common. Ending a minor phrase with a major tonic chord (Tierce de Picardie) is frequently done. There are no key-signatures beyond that of one flat. That is also the case with editions of *Sternhold & Hopkins* or *Ainsworth*. Parallel fifths and octaves were evidently not approved; this may be deduced from their scarcity and from the pains taken to avoid them by crossing the parts or by the use of other legitimate devices. It is difficult to understand why *Este* so often omitted the third of the chord; this omission, however, is found very often in the composers of the William Billings school, i.e. all through the eighteenth century. What was later and is now spoken of as 'false relation' is found often in *Este* and in the writers of the sixteenth and early seventeenth centuries. *Este* has much key-variety within the tune; this is shown if the last two chords in each phrase are taken as cadential.

It was during the reign of James the First (1566-1625) that the migration of the Pilgrims to America took place. As Professor Waldo Selden Pratt states[23]: "the Pilgrims' settlement at Plymouth, Massachusetts, was overshadowed by the larger and more fortunate

---

[22] For harmonic analysis of Psalm 84 see Appendix A.

[23] *The Music of the Pilgrims*, Waldo Selden Pratt, Oliver Ditson Company, Boston, 1921, pp. 80. It will be noted that the harmonizations of sixteen of the tunes are in the style of a later period.

Puritan plantations around Boston to the north, representing a somewhat different set of impulses, though of a related class.[24] Popular thought to-day tends to confound the two undertakings. The times were troublous; the 'Thirty Years War' was being waged; the long reign of Louis Thirteenth was in progress and the mighty Richelieu was at the summit of his power. . . . The religious unrest in France among the Huguenots was soon to culminate in unsuccessful hostilities with Cardinal Richelieu; Protestantism was at a low ebb. The Pilgrims looked longingly to the new world for an expansion of their social and religious ideals. It was the Pilgrims who had their own psalter written by their accomplished doctor or teacher, Henry Ainsworth." We are again indebted to Professor Waldo S. Pratt (op. cit.) for his pamphlet on the Pilgrim psalter. The title given by Ainsworth to the book is *The Book of Psalmes Englished both in Prose/and Metre/with Annotations, opening the words/and sentences, by conference/ with other scriptures./By H. A. . . . Imprinted at Amsterdam/by Giles Thorp/Ao. Di. 1612.* According to the *Encyclopedia Britannica,* article 'Ainsworth, Henry,' he was born about 1571, dying 1622. He was a noted Hebrew scholar and acted for a time as doctor, or teacher, of the reformers under the leadership of Robert Browne (Brownists) who had fled from persecution in England, landing (1620) at what is now Plymouth, Massachusetts. Professor Pratt's pamphlet of eighty pages will be found most valuable, not only in its direct treatment of the *Ainsworth Psalter,* but also in its references to matters musical, social, and religious that help to make a vivid picture of the time immediately preceding and following 1620. Of the thirty tunes in this psalter, eighteen, according to Professor Pratt, are probably French *(Genevan Psalter)* in origin; in fact he assumes with some confidence that much more than a majority of all are French or modified from the French. It seems entirely reasonable, as Professor Pratt writes (pp. 10-11) that "the reformers had, of course, brought from England the 'song-usages'

---

[24] In regard to this point Dr. Percy A. Scholes writes me, "They were Puritans, separated Puritans. The term 'Pilgrims' and 'Puritans' implies a distinction more observed in the United States than in Great Britain, and even so a distinction that concerns a very brief period; for the Puritans (in the American sense) when they came, soon ceased to form a part of the Church of England and when thus 'separated' were practically indistinguishable from the Pilgrims."

that had been gradually forming since the beginning of Queen Elizabeth's reign; the *Ainsworth Psalter* was a unique blend of styles including a large proportion of French forms, and the transplanted vine of song had not the strength to strike root permanently." No doubt the ten-syllabled lines common in the French psalter gave rise to the complaint that the Ainsworth melodies were difficult to sing. At any rate *The Bay Psalm Book*[25] (1640) had little difficulty in supplanting the *Ainsworth Psalter,* though the latter was still in evidence in Salem and Ipswich as late as 1667. *The Bay Psalm Book* tunes were largely in common metre, easily learned if not already known to the Pilgrims from their English experiences, and were not entirely supplanted until 1692.

The Boston Public Library has copies of *Ainsworth Psalter,* editions of 1612 and 1642. These editions are type-set, the staves and diamond-shaped notes are often small, and the C clefs are so tiny as to have made it difficult for the compositor to place them clearly on the proper line; they idly float about the staff as if not sure where they belonged. There are numerous errors. A reading glass is a help. Barlines are used only to separate phrases. Common metre (C.M.) preponderates. Melodies only are printed.

---

[25] The title-page of the ninth edition, music section, reads: *The/Psalms,/Hymns,/ and/Spiritual/Songs/of the/Old and New Testaments faithfully/translated into English Metre.* The work is generally if not invariably referred to as *The Bay Psalm Book.* For photographs of the title-pages of the *Ainsworth Psalter* and *The Bay Psalm Book* see Dr. Percy A. Scholes, op. cit., pp. 257-260.

CHAPTER SIX

Melodies of the Reformation Psalters

Tracing melodies used in modern hymnals to their sources in sixteenth or seventeenth century psalters is dependent on the accessibility of the psalters, patience in investigation, and some critical sharpness. Hardly, however, have we found that our *Old Hundred* was originally the *Old Hundred and Thirty-Fourth,* and attributable (nowadays at least) to Bourgeois, than we push our questions as to melodic origins further back still: What was *Old Hundred* before it was captured and made to do duty as a psalm-tune? Was it specially composed? Were the psalm-tunes in general specially composed, or were they popular melodies appropriated, as in Luther's case, by a greedy Reformer looking for help?

Douen[26] attempts to trace the origins of the melodies of the *Genevan Psalter* of 1562. Though Bourgeois in particular subjected the melodies to rigorous editorial supervision and alteration, it is probable that a certain proportion was drawn from the storehouse of modal or Gregorian mediaeval music and another proportion from the people's music contemporary or old. The whole matter belongs to the specialist and is summed up by Sir Richard Terry,[27] as follows:

"Turning from the psalms to their music, we are confronted with the usual difficulty attending all vernacular hymns of the period, viz. the sources of their tunes. . . . That the bulk of the tunes in this Psalter have not been traced to any known source is not surprising if we remember that in the sixteenth century the line of demarcation between sacred and secular music did not exist. (In fact it never has existed in any other than English-speaking countries, and only there in comparatively modern times.) Just as the courtiers of France sang Clément Marot's psalms to any popular air that took their fancy, so the Huguenots adapted, to their vernacular psalms

---

[26] Op. cit., vol. 1.
[27] *Calvin's First Psalter,* pp. vi-vii.

and canticles, tunes that were already known. They would naturally be attracted to the chorals of the Lutherans, but (as everyone knows) some of the best Lutheran chorals were originally secular songs. They, without doubt, adapted melodies with which the Catholic Church had made them familiar. . . . In the task of collecting tunes for the early metrical psalters, all was fish that came to the compiler's net; the 'popish' origin of a tune (provided it was a popular one) was never allowed to interfere with its adaptation to the new vernacular psalms. . . . The tunes in Calvin's First Psalter (21 in number) are all modal."

We need not be surprised at this point to discover that the reformers under Calvin's leadership were opposed to plain-chant and thought that the Genevan psalm-tunes were superior to it. While the critics of the reform music were well aware of its great popularity, they decried the reform psalm-tunes as trivial, sensuous, and deficient in dignity. Douen, in the second volume of his book, takes the uncompromising Protestant position, placing in strong contrast the musical and religious values of plain-chant and the melodies of the Reformation. The chapter "Influence de la Reforme sur la musique"[28] is too long to quote, but Douen's practical objections as to plain-chant may be summarized. Douen says:

"We do not wish to make a comparison between plain-chant and music; one does not compare completely different things." (p. 333) "The question is not to know if there exist some splendid bits in the chants of the Middle Ages, but rather to know whether the ecclesiastical system which excludes rhythm by itself and combats popular tonality, has assisted art." (p. 334) "Without rhythm melody is nothing and rhythm by itself is something, as one feels from the effect of tambourins." "A melody without rhythm is only an inert thing, an inanimate body to which rhythm alone can give life and movement." Douen goes on to say, "After this one is astonished that such a seeker as M. Fetis should have inclined to the general opinion without examination, and not have seen clearly that, far from having saved the art of the Middle Ages, the Church has on the contrary fettered and distorted it." (P. 332)

Even with all this rather peppery decrial of virtue in plain-chant Douen admits that:

"of all the melodies in the *Genevan Psalter* 36 are in the major

---
[28] Op. cit., vol. II, pp. 315-377.

18

mode, 35 in the minor mode without leading-tone, and 53 less than half, in the antique tonality." (P. 341)

Since Douen has been combating plain-chant because, as he says, it excludes rhythm as such and does not use the popular (that is, the eighteenth century) tonality, it seems inconsistent to praise the Genevan melodies at the expense of plain-chant when he is obliged to admit that nearly half of them are in the antique or modal tonalities.

Anyone wishing to go further into this matter would do well to consult Douen or Henry Expert, the latter giving the melodies of the *Genevan Psalter,* with French text.[29]

The indebtedness of English psalmody to France is significantly shown by the inclusion in English hymnals of quotations from the *Genevan Psalter,* or of borrowings from other French sources.[30]

Turning once more to the use of modal psalm-tunes by the older psalters, Livingston (op. cit.) tabulates the tunes of the *Scottish Metrical Psalter* (1635) by modes as follows: Ionian or major mode, 49 tunes; Aeolian or minor mode, 22; Dorian mode, 21; Phrygian mode, 6; these tunes are scored by Richard R. Terry in his edition of the *Scottish Psalter,* and comparisons with the Livingston edition will prove instructive.

---

[29] See f.n. 14.

[30] Turning to the indexes of authors and sources I find in the *English Hymnal* (1933) 74 titles showing French origin; *Church Hymnary* (1927) gives 49; *Hymns Ancient and Modern* (1924), 31. Taking all the better known psalters, a large proportion of their melodies is obsolete, and a certain proportion of the residue is obsolescent; still, much of it is carried along from generation to generation. This is less true of American than of English hymnals.

CHAPTER SEVEN

Rhythm and Meter of the Reformation Psalters

The early psalmody (Calvin, 1539, 1562; Este, 1592; Ainsworth, 1612; taken as examples) was printed without bar-lines, and on the five-line staff; it was usual to separate the lines of words by a line across the staff; the C clefs were used as happened to be convenient; if any key signature was used it was that of one flat; there were no time signatures. In most cases, however, it is not difficult to determine whether the meter is duple or triple, although the imperfection of a large proportion of the printed music will often present difficult problems. The English and Scottish psalters, on account of the preponderance of D.C.M. and C.M. are easier to divide into measures. To transcribe the melodies of the copies of, for example, *Sternhold & Hopkins* found not infrequently in the great libraries, is often a puzzling task.[31]

It is somewhat surprising to find a proportion of triple meter melodies, like the noble *Old 81st* of the *Day Psalter* or Psalm 77 in the *Este Psalter*. This tune has served W. T. Best for a fine organ piece, *Fantasie on an Old English Psalm Tune*. It may be found in the *English Hymnal* (1933), No. 461; also in *Hymns Ancient and Modern* (1924) No. 439. One need not take too seriously the complaint that triple meter tunes were like a man who had one long and one short leg. The exhilaration and impetus of triple meter are marked.

Were the New England composers sensitive to the four-measure

---

[31] The music is usually type-set; the C clefs are commonly on the third or fourth line and demand great care from the compositor in placing on the very narrow staff; the one flat, B flat, third line of G clef or second space or third space of a C clef, is often misplaced, although it may as often help to save a situation. Very careful study, often with the help of a magnifying glass, constant comparison with other editions (or in the case of the *Genevan Psalter* of 1562, with Henry Expert's modern transcription of it), and unceasing vigilance are necessary.

form? Indeed we might ask the same question regarding the British composers whose better works (*St. Anne's, Windsor, York,* and many others) were potentially a part of the American psalmody. The ballad meter was the principal meter used by the English and Scotch and this was formed by an alternation of an eight and a six-syllable line, extending to four lines (common meter) or to eight lines (double common meter). Long meter, used later, commonly had four lines of eight syllables each. The first line of a syllabic tune in C.M. easily fitted itself to four measures (two syllables to a measure), but the second line worked out as three measures. This alternation was of course true for the rest of a C.M. or D.C.M. stanza. The way out of this was, naturally, to add a measure to the six-syllable lines by prolonging the last note in the line. But we have only occasional evidence that this was ever done; on the other hand it may have been done in practice, through compulsion of the rhythmical sense.

At the time of the hymn revival during the early and middle eighteenth century, purely rhythmic effects began to be liked for their own sake; look, for example, to the long-continued popularity in the New England psalmody of the delightful, foot-moving tune of Handel, from his *Richard the First* called in the Methodist books *Jericho Tune* and in the early American ones, *Extol lation.* The tunes of William Billings and Oliver Holden, and indeed of all the New England composers, were vitally rhythmic in contrast to the staid melodies taken from *Sternhold & Hopkins* the old version (O.V.), *Este, Ravenscroft* and the *Scottish Psalter.*

It should not pass without particular notice that in the triple meter tunes of the old dispensation there was usually a syncopated cadence in the penultimate measure; that is, the melody would be written with a minim (half-note), followed by a semibreve (whole note). This manner of cadence (a) overturned for a moment the regularity of the preceding measures and (b) gave the dominant chord a firm grip with which to usher the final tonic; the primary accent (on first beat) of the measure is momentarily evaded, but the evasion simply gives impetus and force to the key chord when it finally comes. In some of the New England collections—indeed in some of the republications of the *Day* or other psalters, the syncopated cadence has been used in the *Old 81st* for each of the phrases. *Hymns Ancient and Modern* does not in general use the syncopated final cadence, but the *English Hymnal* often does. It is greatly to be regretted that some editors have "corrected" the syncopated final cadence and thus diminished greatly the strength of the ending.

To anyone who has leisure and patience as well as good eyes, and who lives near a great library, the study of the old psalters may become an absorbing recreation. If I may venture to recommend my own experience as a beginner it was this: I took the two copies of the *Ainsworth Psalter* that were available at the Boston Public Library, comparing them psalm by psalm with each other, and checking results note by note with Professor Pratt, (op. cit.). He has given the whole of the melodies in modern notation, with one stanza of the psalm to which a melody is intended to be sung, and notes historical and musical; at the end of the book there are harmonizations by himself of sixteen of the melodies. These comparisons will be an effective initiation into the misbehavior of the C clef and the difference in regard to note-length of the various editions that may be consulted.

Prayer books of the sixteenth century with melodies for the Psalms may be studied to advantage. A good example is Sir Thomas Fairfax's *Edward VIth Prayer Book,* 1581.[32] On the title page is 'Arise for it is Day' the last word being spelled on last page 'Daye'. The paper is thin with vertical watermarks, about nine to a page, and seven eighths of an inch apart. The printing shows through, though not to hinder reading. The music is typeset, staves about seven eighths of an inch wide. There are five kinds of notes. There is a sign used both as a rest and to divide phrases. The notes are sometimes dotted. The airs are printed in one continuous strain; when harmonized the air is in the tenor. The only key-signature used is that of one flat, F major (D minor), but we may assume that the airs were transposed to conform to the conditions of performance. It must be remembered that the modern consciousness of a series of tonalities nicely adjusted to cycles of keys was not fully developed before J. S. Bach, b. 1685. The notes of the airs do not accommodate themselves customarily to the

---

[32] Boston Public Library, No. 3 in Benton 2.2: bound up with a *Sternhold & Hopkins,* 1580.

later four-measure phrase structure; indeed there were no measures, although singers evidently felt the appeal of the balancing
of phrases of equal length in point of duration. This is perhaps
more true here than of the *Genevan Psalter* (1562) tunes, since
their stanza-lines were of a great variety of lengths, whereas the
English Psalter gave great prominence to the ballad meter. The
rules for MSS as regards the turning up and down of stems of notes
were as they are today. The 'direct' is a feature of the *Fairfax
Psalter*, used at the end of one line to indicate the note beginning the succeeding line; and at the end of the page a word to
show the first word on the next page. Since the meter of the melodies did not have to accommodate itself to a rigorous feeling for
four-measure phrases, and since the mediaeval system of modes
was losing its hold, there must have been a certain give-and-take
in performance, quite in contrast to the modern exactness. Often
the performer feels obliged to use *musica ficta*[33] to supply inflections of the notes that he feels are demanded. All this tonal and
rhythmical flexibility probably gave to the longer Genevan melodies especially, something of the unworldiness, the veiled and
mystical beauty that is characteristic of plain-song; though on the
other hand the development of rhythm and harmony came from
the Reformation music, rather than from the mediaeval plain-
song.[34]

---

[33] See *Grove's Dictionary of Music and Musicians,* Third Edition, Macmillan and
Company, Ltd., 1927, article "Musica ficta"; or *Contrapuntal Technique,* R. C. Mor-
ris, Clarendon Press, Oxford, 1922, pp. 10, 11.

[34] See Chapter V in *A Grammar of Plainsong,* the Benedictines of Stanbrook,
Burnes and Oates, Ltd., London, 1905.

CHAPTER EIGHT

The Influence of Thomas Ravenscroft, John Playford, Tate and Brady on New England Psalmody

Plymouth and Boston are the main focal points in the study of New England psalmody. It is true that towns like Salem, Ipswich, Sudbury, Dedham, Medfield, Framingham and others that might be named were comparatively large centers of social and political interest. Today, however, it is natural to associate Plymouth with the settlement of the Pilgrims on Cape Cod, and Boston with the somewhat later advent of the more aristocratic Puritans on Massachusetts Bay.

Palfrey, the historian of New England,[35] writes:

"The founders of the commonwealths of which I write were Englishmen. Their migration to New England began in 1620. It was inconsiderable until 1630. At the end of ten years more it almost ceased. A people, consisting at that time of not many more than twenty thousand persons, thenceforward multiplied on its own soil, in remarkable seclusion from other communities, for nearly a century and a half."

Later on he remarks that:

"a religious impulse accomplished what commercial enterprise, commanding money and court favor had attempted without success."

On p. 157 of vol. ii, op. cit. there is a description by Winslow of the setting off by the Pilgrims from Delft-Haven to take the ship *Speedwell* to their new homes. "When the ship was ready to carry us away," says Winslow, "the brethren that stayed having solemnly sought the Lord with us and for us . . . feasted us at our pastor's

---

[35] *History of New England*, Little, Brown and Co., Boston, 1858, vol. 1, p. vii.

24

house, being large, where we refreshed ourselves, after tears, with singing of psalms, making joyful melody in our hearts as well as with the voice, there being many of the congregation very expert in music." It seems that the Pilgrims enjoyed singing. The tunes they sang may have been from the *Ainsworth Psalter* (1612), which they took with them to the New World; from the *Sternhold & Hopkins Psalter,* nearly sixty years old at this date, or from the *Este Psalter.* It is a very pleasant picture made by this little band of psalm-singers, despite the tears and forebodings. As to the latter, they may possibly have sung the old twenty-fourth psalm set to the stirring triple-meter tune in *Ainsworth* with the D.C.M. stanzas beginning:

"Lift up, ye gates, your heads and ye
Dores of eternal aye,
Be lifted up that so the King
Of glory enter may."

That tune would have set them right. It is the same tune that Calvin had used for Psalm 68 in his psalter of 1562, the Scots for Psalm 77 and the English, in their *Sternhold & Hopkins* of the same date. This tune as well as many others had been a common heritage of the Reformers both in and out of the Church of England. Of course, *Ainsworth* (1612) was their own special property and they took his *Psalter* with them to the New World and used it until the 'new' *(Tate & Brady) Whole Book of Psalms* came out in 1696, just before the seventeen-hundreds.

Even as late as 1730, in Saco, Maine,[36] it is reported:

"that most congregations could sing five tunes with greater or less harmony, and sometimes in a congregation whose membership included accomplished singers, the number could be extended to ten tunes. The favorite tunes were *York, Hackney, Martyrs,* and *Windsor.* They were sung without instrumental accompaniment."

What psalm-tunes did the Pilgrims and Puritans use in their worship? Coffin's *History of Newbury* declares, "five tunes are the maximum number any congregation could sing." These five were *Hackney, Martyrs, St. Mary's,*[37] *Windsor* and *York.* Curwen's

---

[36] See p. 12 in *Music and Musicians of Maine,* G. T. Edwards, 1925.
[37] But *Hackney* and *St. Mary's* are the same tune.

Studies in Worship Music, London, 1880, vol. I, mentions "only five or six tunes sung up to 1680", namely *Litchfield, Martyrs, Oxford, St. David's, Windsor* and *York*. H. W. Foote writes:[38]

> "Our forefathers had brought with them from England five tunes; and these perpetuated not by written notes but by tradition, continued for a long time to be the only ones used."

Foote strangely overlooks the fact that the Pilgrims brought with them from Holland the *Ainsworth Psalter,* their own particular property, published in 1612 at Amsterdam, and this had thirty-nine tunes. The *Day Psalter* had been in use in England for fifty-eight years, and it would be strange if it had not, even though indirectly, given the Pilgrims help in their singing; they left Scrooby for Holland as early as 1608, which would mean that they, being without the Ainsworth book of psalms, would be forced to use the *Day Psalter*. It seems unreasonable to suppose that from force of circumstances the Pilgrims had only five tunes at their command, and if it is objected that they were probably unskilled in music I will recall Winslow's statement, "there being many of the congregation very expert in music." Taking into account the English and the Ainsworth psalters there was material enough for the singing of many more than five tunes. It would be unfair to carry further the argument based upon abundance of material, for it is generally recognized that congregations today know only a small part of the tunes in their collections. Still, until we have some sort of contemporary evidence that the early settlers in New England sang only five tunes, we shall continue to think the statement unfounded, at any rate as regards the settlers around Massachusetts Bay.

To the *Day, Este,* and *Ainsworth* psalters we must add the work of Thomas Ravenscroft (1621), the *Whole Book of Psalmes*; and John Playford's collection (1677). These five collections were, in time, accessible to the American colonists and from their store of fine melody were taken many of the tunes in the 1698 edition of *The Bay Psalm Book,* the first edition of that famous book to include melodies. We should mention here Reverend John Tufts's *Intro-*

---

[38] *Annals of King's Chapel,* 1895.

duction (1721); this is a fine collection, and if looked at as a reflection of Colonial taste in selection, is noteworthy.

The title page of *Playford* reads in part: "*The Whole Book/of Psalmes/with the Usual Hymns and spiritual Songs/together with all the Ancient and proper tunes sung/in church, with some of later use./Composed in three parts/Cantus, Medius, and Bassus/in a more plain and Useful method than hath been formerly, published by John Playford, 1677.*" This psalter was designed to answer two main purposes: to make a simpler arrangement of the tunes as they appeared in *Ravenscroft,* and therefore to revive the interest in psalm-singing. The twentieth edition was published in 1757 and it is said that the work's influence extended in all for over a hundred years. The three-part arrangement was helpful in the matter of ease of execution.

Playford writes: "the Church Tone is placed in the treble part[39] (which is the cantus, with the bass under it) as most proper to joyn voice and instruments together, according to David's prescription, Psalm 144,9. And since many of our churches are lately furnished with organs, it will also be useful for the organist and likewise for such students in the universities as shall practice Song, to a Lute or Violl. The medius part is composed (as is) proper not to rise above the Church Tone, to cloud or obscure the ayre thereof, except in such places as could not well be avoided." It seems to me plain that Playford was not in sympathy with the crossing of the voices even if it was more or less an inheritance from the Elizabethan period. Playford omits to say that when sung by men the medius part should be sung an octave lower than written. It is easy to assume that voices of medium pitch, both of men and women, sing the medius. Playford continues: "the bass is composed in such a compass of notes as will suit an indifferent voice both below and above. All three parts may be sung by men as properly by boys and women: and to that end the two upper parts in the G solreut clef and the bass in the F faut (the proper) clef."

In passing it is not without interest to remark that both the 'old'

---

[39] Playford made a point of placing the air on the highest of the three staves (Cantus), "all parts," as he quaintly adds, "moving together in solemn way of counterpoint." William Damon (London, 1591) had done this, but his example was not followed. James Lyon in *Urania* (1761) has the melody in the Tenor.

(Sternhold & Hopkins) and the 'new' *(Tate & Brady)* psalters were the result of a partnership of authors. Tate was educated in Dublin and afterwards settled in London. Much to everyone's surprise William III made him Poet Laureate, and he lived to write a birthday ode for George I.[40] The attempts to give currency to the *Tate & Brady* version were not sympathetically received. I quote from Dr. Scholes, op. cit., p. 264:

> "As in every instance when an attempt is made to change settled church habits, there was great opposition to the introduction of the new version, and, as has already been seen, although the 'new' was before the public in the days of William and Mary, the 'old' had not quite gone out of vogue when Queen Victoria was a girl. Probably the 'old' did not completely succumb until the competition had been going on for about one hundred and fifty years—by which time its upstart rival, the Tate and Brady, was itself approaching its end. In one of Cowper's letters there is a reference to the rivalry, as experienced in his day. He says that nearly every parish clerk now 'picks his staves out of the New Version', but that in some places the congregation have left the clerk 'to bawl by himself', not having the version at the end of their prayer-book, 'while others are highly disgusted at the innovation'."

The new version had no music, but in 1700 a supplement was issued containing a selection of tunes from earlier psalters, with additions of canticles, some hymns, etc. A page of 'directions', not numbered, gives *York, Windsor, St. David's, Litchfield, Canterbury, Martyrs, Southwell, St. Mary's* alias *Hackney Tune,* as the most usual tunes.[41]

In passing it might be noted that the metrical psalms were never officially admitted to the English Church; it may be guessed that they were first introduced by those in sympathy with the Reformers and afterwards continued by connivance: they never received

---

[40] J. T. Lightwood, op. cit., p. 82.

[41] See *Tate & Brady,* in Hartford Theological Seminary Foundation library, edition of 1698. An edition, 1708, in the Hartford Foundation library, No. 56767, 6th edition, pp. x, 60, is of much value. The tunes are for melody and bass; they are adapted to a variety of metres and there are tunes for the *Te Deum, Veni Creator,* etc. The instructions for singers name 'six several cheerful keys', C, B flat, A, F, G, and D major; and 'six several mournful keys', A, B, C, D, E, and G minor. The older books would have referred to these two groups as "sharp" and "flat keys" respectively. The notes are diamond shape. This 6th edition has sixty tunes, for air and bass.

royal approbation or parliamentary sanction. Notwithstanding, it is said in their title pages that they are "set forth and allowed to be sung in all churches of the people." They were usually bound up with the Prayer Books.[42]

---

[42] Consult Warton, vol. iv, p. 138; Lightwood and *Historical edition* of *Hymns Ancient and Modern* on these points. Dr. Scholes writes me that "the printing of the music in the Prayer Books must have been more than 'connived at.'"

Title-Page of

THE BAY PSALM BOOK

Ninth Edition

The First Edition Having Music

1698

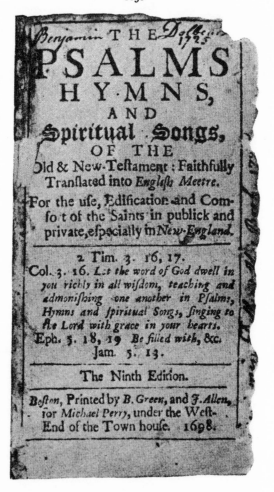

THE

PSALMS

H Y·M N S,

AND

Spiritual Songs,

OF THE

Old & New-Teftament : Faithfully
Tranflated into *Englifh Meetre.*

For the ufe, Edification and Com-
fo t of the Saints in publick and
private,efpecially in *New-England.*

2 Tim. 3. 16, 17.
Col. 3. 16. *Let the word of God dwell in
you richly in all wifdom, teaching and
admonifhing one another in Pfalms,
Hymns and fpiritual Songs, finging to
the Lord with grace in your hearts.*
Eph. 5. 18, 19 *Be filled with,* &c.
Jam. 5. 13.

The Ninth Edition.

Bofton, Printed by *B. Green,* and *J. Allen,*
for *Michael Perry,* under the Weft-
End of the Town houfe. 1698.

30

CHAPTER NINE

The Bay Psalm Book

As Massachusetts established the first college in North America, so it set up the first printing press. It was in January, 1639, that the press procured in England by Reverend Jesse Glover was established in Cambridge, Massachusetts, by direction of the magistrates and elders as an 'appendage of Harvard College.' It was not until 1664 that permission was obtained to set up a press in Boston. When Mr. Glover died the press fell into the possession of his wife; and upon her marriage to Reverend Henry Dunster, the first President of Harvard College, the press was placed under his supervision, remaining in his house until 1665. The first works printed on this press were the *Freeman's Oath, Peirce's Almanac,* and (1640) the *Psalms newly turned into metre.*[43] The metrical version of the psalms was not altogether approved and a revised version was ordered under the oversight of President Dunster and first printed in 1650. This was *The Bay Psalm Book,*[44] which speedily came into use in the New England churches and obtained a wide circulation in England and Scotland, passing through seventy editions at home and abroad; the last edition was issued in 1773. It was used in England as late as 1754, the eighteenth edition, and in Scotland, as late as 1759, twenty-second edition. The formal title of the first edition (without music) was:[45] *"The/ Whole/Booke of Psalmes/Faithfully/Translated into English/ Metre/Whereunto is prefixed a discourse de/claring not only the lawfulness, but also/the necessity of the heavenly ordinance/of singing Scripture Psalmes/in the Churches/of God/ . . . 1640."*

---

[43] See *Life of Henry Dunster,* Rev. Jeremiah Chaplin, Boston, J. R. Osgood & Co., 1872, pp. 91-96, 97-100. Also Palfrey, *History of New England,* vol. II, p. 41 footnote. Also Curwen, *Studies in Worship Music,* 1880, p. 57.

[44] Dr. P. A. Scholes, op. cit., pp. 259-260.

[45] A literal reprint made for Charles B. Richardson, without music, appeared in New York in 1862; a copy is in the Boston Public Library.

It may be described as, "Small 8 vol. Upright, two and one half by five and one half inches." No music was included until the ninth edition in 1698. A significant note at the end of this edition states:

> "the verses of the psalmes may be reduced to six kinds, the first whereof may be sung in very neere fourty common tunes, as they are collected out of our chief musicians by Tho. Ravenscroft."

The Puritans did not make an easy matter of reducing the psalms to meter or of singing them when so paraphrased. The book may be quoted on these points.

> "There have been three questions especially stirring concerning singing. First, what psalmes are to be sung in churches. Whether David's and other scripture psalmes or the psalmes invented by the gift of godly men in every age of the church. Secondly, if Scripture Psalmes, whether in their own words or in such meeter as English poetry is wont to run in. Thirdly, by whom are they to be sung? Whether by the whole churches together with their voices? Or by one man singing alone and the rest joining in silence, and in the close singing 'amen'."

As to 'meeter' we read:

> "there are many verses together in several psalmes of David which run in rithmes . . . which shows at least the lawfulness of singing psalmes in English rithmes."

Again quoting from the reprint, it is worth while noting that 'been', a word whose pronunciations in England and the United States are different, was pronounced in New England in 1640 much as it is today. The stanza following is apropos:

> "Thou hast put gladness in my heart,
>   more than time wherein
>   their corne, and also their new wine,
>   have much increased bin."

The 13 tunes in the ninth edition of *The Bay Psalm Book* are noted below; they appeared with melody and bass only. The engraving is clear up to *Martyr's Tune,* and there is uniformity in the size of the diamond-shaped notes; the notes in treble and bass, sounding together, were on the same vertical line; in *Martyr's*

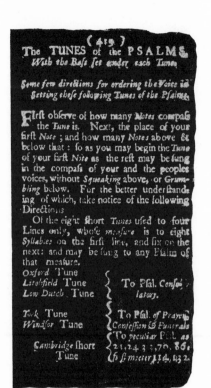

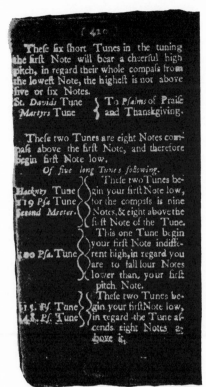

When the singing of the psalms was unaccompanied (which must have been often the case), pitching the tune was a matter of much delicacy, resulting in humiliating failures if the tune was started too high or two low. The tuning-fork was not invented until 1711.[46]

There were thirteen tunes in the ninth edition; of these eight tunes (*Oxford, Hackney* or *St. Mary, Canterbury, York, Windsor, Ps. 100, Ps. 119,* and *Ps. 148*) appeared later in both Tufts's *Introduction*, 1726, and Walter's *Grounds and Rules.*

The tunes are all for Treble and Bass.

[46] See Grove, op. cit., article "Tuning Fork."

Psalm 4—*Oxford Tune*

The first and third lines are the treble part; below are the bass notes. The metre is 8.6.8.6. or common metre (ballad metre). The letters under the notes are the first letters of the sol-fa syllables of the major scale, fa, sol, la, fa, sol, la, mi, fa. *F* and *f* sharp are treated for sol-faing as if the same pitch, i.e. as if the key were *f* major and not *g* minor. The *x* is the sharp, and the flat is the round-head, sign. The sharp after the 20th Treble note ought to appear before it. *Oxford Tune* is found in Ravenscroft's *Whole Book of Psalms* (1621), Walter's *Grounds* (1721), Tufts's *Introduction* (1726) and as late as 1756 in *Tate & Brady*.

Psalm 69—*Lichfield Tune* (also *Litchfield*). Called *London* in Tufts's *Introduction*. It is a different tune in Walter's *Grounds*. Ravenscroft's *Lichfield* is a different tune. The sol-fa syllables are those of *F* major scale. The bass notes are never a fourth from the treble, only a third, fifth or octave.

Psalm 23—*Low Dutch Tune*, the third C. M. tune of this page, is found in *Este* (1592) for Psalm 4; it is later called *Canterbury*. Found in Tufts's *Introduction* and Walter's *Grounds*.

Each of the three tunes presents interesting problems worth study.

Tune the verticals are quite disregarded and the note heads vary a good deal in size, showing a difference in engravers.

The order of tunes is as follows: *Oxford,* G minor, duple time, Psalm 4; *Lichfield,* G minor, duple time, Psalm 69; *Low Dutch Tune,* G major, duple time, Psalm 23; *York,* F major, duple time, Psalm 73; *Windsor,* G minor, duple time, Psalm 118; *Cambridge Short Tune,* G minor, duple time, Psalm 70; *St. David's,* F major, duple time, Psalm 99; *Martyrs,* G minor, duple time, Psalm 39 (modal); *Hackney,* D minor, duple time, *Psalm 61;* Second Meeter, Double common meter, E minor, *Psalm 119;* First Meeter, G major, duple time, *Psalm 100;* First Meeter, Long meter, 8 lines, G major, duple time, *Psalm 115;* First Meeter, Short meter, C major, duple time, *Psalm 148.*[46]

---

[46] While it is not difficult in some of these tunes to show modal influence *Martyrs* is the most striking example of it. See No. 520 in *The Church Hymnal,* 1933 and No. 449 in *The English Hymnal,* 1906. No. 125 in *Hymns Ancient and Modern,* historical edition, has a perversion of the tune.

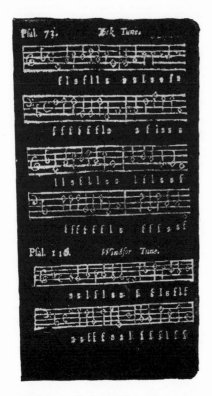

Psalm 73—*York* or *The Stilt* is first found in *The Cl Psalms of David*, Edinburgh, 1615, under the second name, explained as a melodic imitation in the first and third phrases of the alternate motion of the legs in walking on stilts. *York* has had an honorable history up to the present time. Attention is called to the dot at the side of the last note in the first phrase as used in the modern way for the prolongation of a note. The natural (x) not in general use, as shown in phrase two.

Psalm 116—*Windsor Tune* is found in *Este* (1592), and in the later psalters; in the *Scottish Psalter* (1635) it is called *Dundie (Dundee)*. The English tune, *Dundee*, is a different tune and in Scotland is known as *French*.

Psalm 70—*Cambridge Short Tune*. The meter is 6.6.8.6. Another *Cambridge* is 8.6.8.6. The two tunes have a certain small resemblance. The 6.6.-8.6. form (1679) is now called *London* or *Southwell*. (See *Hymns Ancient and Modern*, hist. edn., 462.)

For *St. David's*, see next illustration.

36

CHAPTER TEN

The Ministers, John Tufts, Thomas Walter, and James Lyon

I. The Reverend John Tufts
(May 5, 1689—August, 1750)

It is not uncommon to find directions for 'tuning the voice' in connection with the appendix of tunes at the end of the psalters, but Tufts's *Introduction* was probably the first collection of tunes in New England to give systematic instruction in reading notes.

John Tufts was a native of Medford, Massachusetts. Graduating from Harvard College in 1708 he served as pastor in Charlestown and afterwards in Newbury; in 1738 he left Newbury and removed to Amesbury, where he spent the rest of his life.[47]

Tufts's modest manual was published in the early part of the eighteenth century. There seems to be some doubt as to the date of the first edition. Metcalf (op. cit.) speaks of it as "given by different writers as between 1714 and 1721." The Allen A. Brown Collection in the Boston Public Library has copies of the 1726 (fifth) edition, and the tenth.[48]

The tunes were scored[49] in three lines, the top line, G clef, has the Cantus or air; the middle line, G clef, is Medius, often writ-

---

[47] For fuller particulars of Tufts's life see Appendix B, and F. J. Metcalf's *American Writers and Compilers of Sacred Music*, The Abingdon Press, Boston, 1925; pp. 16-18.

[48] Of the 37 tunes that Tufts collected the *Church Hymnary* (1927) has eight, namely *Martyr's, Commandments, St. Michaels, St. David's, St. Mary's, Windsor, Gloucester,* and *St. James'*. The *English Hymnal* (1933) has the same ones except *Gloucester*. The *Hymnal* (1934), published by the General Assembly of the Presbyterian Church in the United States, has *St. James'* only. The *Pilgrim Hymnal* (1931), Boston, has none of them. The *New Hymnal* (1916), Episcopalian, United States has *St. Michael's, Windsor, St. James'*. The longevity of these tunes is the strongest proof of their merit. See also Appendix C.

[49] See "Multiplicity of Methods of Scoring", p. 95 in Chapter XVII.

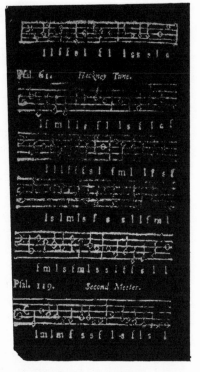

Psalm 95—*St. David's Tune* (see preceding illustration for first line of treble) as printed here was modified by Playford (1677). First in Ravenscroft (1621). (See *Hymns Ancient and Modern*, hist. edn. 542.)

Psalm 39—*Martyrs,* a tune in the Doric mode, has persisted in holding a place in modern psalmody. (*Church Hymnary,* No. 520; *English Hymnal,* No. 449.) The third and fourth phrases of the bass will be found over the *Hackney Tune,* q.v. *Martyrs* is first found in *The CL Psalms of David,* A. Hart, Edinburg, 1615.

Psalm 61—*Hackney Tune* or *St. Mary's* is first found in Archdeacon Prys's *Welsh Psalter* (1621). The first note in the third phrase is A. In *Church Music Reformed* (1765) John Arnold calls *St. Mary's, Martyrs* and *London Old* bad tunes.

See next illustration for Psalm 119, second meeter.

ten an octave higher than sung; and the bottom line for the Bass (F clef). This was a John Playford (1677) style of score.

Tufts used the five-line staff; instead of the diamond-shaped notes he placed the initial letters of the sol-fa syllables *fa, sol, la, mi* on the appropriate lines and spaces; there were two sorts of notes indicating time, the longer note with a dot side of it, and the shorter note unmarked in that way. The sol-fa syllables referred to above had an important part to play in reading music, and the seventh of the scale, called 'mi', was the important note in it.[50] This method took little or no account of keys and key-relationships in the sense in which we understand those matters, and this seems to have inevitably complicated their solmization. It will be noted that the syllables *fa-sol-la* were applied both to the first, second and third as well as to the fourth, fifth and sixth sounds of the scale. This ambiguity must have muddled many weak brains, although it would have done the singing-school master's business no harm. I defy any twentieth-century musician to take a page of the GROUNDS (rudiments of music as we say now) and, on first or second reading, get any clear idea as to "what it's all about."

There was uncertainty as to the kind of voice that should sing the medius and counter used in the larger score; also, whether the music should be sung as written or an octave lower. The *C* clef was a help in such cases, since it indicated the exact pitch.

Crossing by the higher voices was resorted to rather more than less, and this tended to obscure the melody, a result which was also brought about by the uncertainty as to the voices that should sing the tenor, restricted up to 1677 to the men's voices, the women finding their proper part in the treble. Tufts, however, following John Playford, writes the tune in the top line, that is, the cantus, expecting the treble voices to sing it.

II. The Reverend Thomas Walter
(December 7, 1696—January 10, 1725)

In Metcalf's *American Writers and Compilers* there is a sketch of the Reverend Thomas Walter, the author of the *Grounds and Rules of Music* explained. See also *Dictionary of American Bi-*

---

[50] See "Solmization," Appendix N.

Psalm 119, Second Meeter. For the first and second phrases of the treble, see preceding illustration; the fourteenth treble note should follow the sharp. In James Lyon's *Urania* (1761) called *The old 119th psalm*. A comparison with the version in the *Scottish Psalter* (1635) will show differences. The two final phrases of the bass will be found on the top of the r.h. music. The meter is D.C.M. (8.6.8.6.8.6.8.6.)

Psalm 100. First Meeter. In the *Genevan Psalter* (1551) set to Psalm 134. In *Este* (1592) to Psalm 100. *The Scottish Psalter* (1635), all phrases, treble, has long notes for the first, sixth, seventh, and eighth notes. In addition, the second and third notes of the treble, fourth phrase, are also long. *Sternhold & Hopkins* (1562) and *Este*, differ from the *Scottish Psalter* in note-lengths. The meter is L. M. (8.8.8.8.)

40

Psalm 115, First Meeter. (L.M. 8.8.-8.8.) For two first phrases in treble see bottom of preceding page.

Sharping the C was a common error. *Este* has the C natural, and assigns the air to Psalm 113. The *Scottish Psalter* (1635) has the C natural and the attribution to Psalm 113. The tune takes care of a twelve-line stanza, that is, a stanza of twelve phrases; the treble of the tenth and eleventh phrases is missing, although their bass is the top line of the next illustration. (For the missing notes see *Hymns Ancient and Modern,* Historical Edition, p. 457, or any recent hymnal.)

Psalm 148, First Meeter. Probably *Sternhold & Hopkins.* In *Scottish Psalter* (1635) as Psalm 136. It is Psalm 108 in the *Ainsworth Psalter.*

The music is incomplete; the 9th edition used is in the Massachusetts Historical Society library.

ography.[51] F. W. Colburn, author of the article on Walter, op. cit., dubs him the defender of the new way of singing, thus cleverly summing up Walter's book. The various editions are April 18, 1721; 1723; 1740; 1760; 1764.

Walter was born in Roxbury, Massachusetts; his father was the Reverend Nehemiah Walter of Irish ancestry, his mother, Sarah Mather, daughter of Increase Mather. Walter graduated from Harvard brilliantly with an A.M. in 1713; in 1718 he was ordained as his father's assistant in Roxbury; he married Rebeckah Belcher, daughter of Reverend Joseph Belcher. An only daughter survived him.

As a boy he was distinguished for a retentive memory. C. K. Dillaway writes:[52]

> "There was no subject but what Walter was intimately acquainted with. . . . He was distinguished for his musical taste; and the author of an elementary work on the science of music which became very popular. The tunes he collected were introduced into our churches and his rules taught in our schools."

Colburn, op. cit., is of the opinion that:

> "simple as was the musical technique involved, this book stood for an effort, scientifically and artistically conceived, to correct what Walter called, 'an horrid medley of confused and disorderly sounds'."

Quoting from the preface of the 1746 edition, it would seem that nothing could be spoken in praise or even defense of the singing in New England churches at the time:

> ". . . once the tunes were sung according to the rules of music, but are now miserably tortured and twisted. . . . There are no two churches that sing alike. . . . Somebody or other did compose our tunes, and did they, think ye? compose them by rule or by rote? If the latter how came they pricked down in our Psalm books? . . . For want of exactitude, I have observed in many places one man is upon one note, while another a note behind, which produces something hideous and beyond expression bad."

---

[51] Vol. xix, p. 395, states that the best connected account of Thomas Walter is by C. F. Adams, Jr., in *Notices of the Walter Family, New England Historical & Genealogical Register*, July, 1854.

[52] *History of the Grammar School in Roxbury*, Boston, 1860.

Even if we allow for Walter's undoubted fastidiousness his strictures seem intemperate and censorious. Perhaps what Walter really wanted to say was that he thought the music in the churches was in much need of improvement!

III. The Reverend James Lyon[53]
(July 1, 1735–October 12, 1794)

James Lyon's *Urania* was published in 1761; it was "A choice collection of psalm-tunes, anthems and hymns." Oscar G. Sonneck contributed a detailed and valuable discussion of *Urania* in his *Hopkinson and Lyon*.[54] Lyon was a contemporary of Hopkinson, wrote a graduation ode at Princeton University (1759), and composed several anthems, which are distinguished by asterisms, appearing in his collection. In size, general appearance and workmanship *Urania* was considerably superior to any of the musical works preceding it, the whole work testifying to his good taste in several directions; it is oblong in form, numbers pages xii-198, measures 9¼ inches by 4¼ inches, and is engraved throughout in a consistently clear style.

There are twelve pages of explanation of the gamut; the English time-distinctions, as breve, crotchet, quaver, are used, the major scale appearing in the guise of *fa, sol, la, fa, sol, la, mi, fa*. The seventy psalm-tunes are in four-line score, treble, counter, tenor and bass; the air, for men's voices, is in the tenor. Colonial purists were much troubled by the insistence of some of the women in singing the air, instead of minding their own business and working with the treble line.

A striking feature of *Urania* was the inclusion of fourteen hymns with their accompanying tunes. The tunes in the Tufts and Walter collections were strictly psalm-tunes, although they were, of course, equally adapted as time went on to the hymns of the same metre. Some discussion has arisen from the use by Lyon of the air known in England as early as 1745 as a national anthem; Lyon names it *Whitefield*.[55] It remains for a sufficiently earnest

---

[53] See Appendix D.
[54] *Frances Hopkinson and James Lyon, two studies in early American music.* O. G. Sonneck, Washington, D. C., 1905, pp. 209.
[55] See Grove, op. cit., topic "God Save the King."

43

The illustrations are from the Boston Public Library copy, fifth edition. The pages are a marvel of clearness in condensation and accuracy; they will repay study. The music follows John Playford's example (1677) in a three-line score, with the air on the top line. The dot at the side of a capital letter (which stands for a scale-sound) doubles its length; the curved line (slur) functions as in modern hymn-tunes. The harmony of the tunes is in general correct and strong, although going little beyond the root position and first inversion of the principal chords in the key.

soul to determine how this tune was given this name. Had the name any connective association with the evangelist, George Whitefield, who visited America the first time in 1739 and several times later? The words furnished for *Whitefield* are the well-known hymn beginning, "Come Thou, Almighty King"; the second stanza of *Urania* reads:

> "Jesus, our Lord, arise
> Scatter our enemies
> And make them fall."

which closely allies itself with the second stanza of "God Save the King," reading:

> "O Lord, our God arise
> Scatter his enemies
> And make them fall."

Curious—perhaps more curious than significant. O. G. Sonneck[56] states that:

"James Lyon used English publications more freely than American (Bay Psalm Book, Tufts, Walter). In particular he borrowed from the *Divine Musical Miscellany* and from the collections of Arnold, Greene, Knapp, Evison, but not from Tans'ur. The extent to which he copied the favorite English psalmodists of the day shows how well he had studied their works. Unless his acquaintance with English psalmody was exceptional in the Colonies it would be of singular importance as proving the lively intercourse between Great Britain and the British in America in musical matters."

Two anthems, distinguished by asterisms, *The Lord descended from above* and *Let the shrill trumpet's warlike voice*, point out original compositions by Lyon. Sonneck, op. cit., p. 193-4, appraises Lyon's value as a composer:

"Lyon was not a composer of real merit; his music is in no ways remarkable, his 'Friendship' being his best piece.[57] Lyon energetically busied himself with music when music was in its infancy in Colonial

---

[56] Sonneck, O. G., op. cit., p. 177.
[57] Sonneck, op. cit., p. 108, prints a rather more than interesting programme given in Philadelphia in May, 1786; it included the two anthems noted above and Billings's *Rose of Sharon*. The piece *Friendship* may be found in Elias Mann's *Massachusetts Collection of Sacred Harmony*, 1807, pp. 170-4.

45

America, in response to inborn musical talent. Not the absolute but the relative value of his music attracts our attenion. He was a pioneer and thereupon rests his lasting glory. . . . But what are we allowed to expect from James Lyon if even the British models of our early psalmodists were still laden with the cruel burden of mi-fa, the crux in musica, and still trying to reconcile an antiquated system of music with exigencies grown out of 'vertical' music?"

In external appearance *Urania* contrasts favorably with the works of Billings of the same date. It would be a pleasure to see a copy of *Urania* fresh from engraver, printer and binder, the note heads exactly the same size, stems of notes turned consistently up and down, the notes that are to be sounded together on the same vertical line, and the bar-lines vertically placed. Nothing crowded, title-page handsome, clefs carefully placed on the correct line, sharps and flats and meter figures unmistakable: a handsome production.

In coldly appraising Lyon's anthems as music, taking into account the standards of musicianship illustrated by *Ravenscroft*, the *Scottish Psalter* of 1635, or even the psalm-tunes of the ambitious but minor William Tans'ur, we have little to praise. Sonneck is of the opinion that Lyon was well acquainted with the current English psalmody, but there is no evidence that he had profited thereby. A superficial examination of any page of *Urania* convicts its compiler of gross ignorance of what then, as now, were the simplest technical procedures. For my part Lyon's music represents the effort of a young, enthusiastic, naturally talented music pupil who ought to have been studying the first principles of chord connection; and yet I must add that, taken all in all, *Urania* is more than a case of one running before being sent.

Frontispiece, THE NEW ENGLAND PSALM-SINGER

"A Canon of 6 in one" is from the frontispiece of *The New England Psalm-Singer* (1770). We note seven singers, or six singers and a director, at the left. Mr. William H. Capen of Stoughton, Massachusetts, president of the Stoughton Musical Society, formed in 1786, tells me that there is an unwritten somewhat tenuous tradition that the figure at the left was intended for Billings himself. Persistent search by Mr. Capen has failed to find any sketch, painting, drawing or attempt at a portrait of Billings. The attribution on the right, "P. Revere Sculp," will attract the reader's attention.

CHAPTER ELEVEN

William Billings

(October 7, 1746—September 28, 1800)

"William Billings, often erroneously called 'the first American composer', was an uneducated man of humble birth, by trade a tanner, who had an irrepressible enthusiasm for developing popular singing."[58]

"William Billings was a giant among the group of composers who flourished in New England during the period of the Revolutionary War. He towered above those around him, and planted the impress of his power upon those who attempted to follow in his footsteps. His style of music has been held up to ridicule. Few of his pieces are now in common use, but this is only another instance of the constant change in musical taste, and a desire for new compositions which displace the old."[59]

"He (Billings) was just then at the zenith of his career. His *New England Psalm-Singer* of 1770 and his *Singing Master's Assistant* of 1778, and later collections of his hymns and psalm-tunes had attracted—not for their musical grammar, which was conspicuously absent, but for the undeniable spark of something akin to originality—attention to his name wherever psalms were sung in the Northern and Middle States, and hardly a single psalm-tune collection by the American psalmodists of this period is to be found in which Billings' Muse does not prominently figure. In short, his name and fame resounded in the remotest church choir and without doubt he was the most popular composer of his day."[60]

The most informing sketch of William Billings's life is that given by F. J. Metcalf, op. cit., pp. 51-64.

---

[58] *Grove's Dictionary of Music, American Supplement*, ed. by Waldo Selden Pratt and Charles N. Boyd, Theodore Presser Co., Philadelphia, 1923.

[59] Frank J. Metcalf, op. cit.

[60] O. G. Sonneck, *Early Concert Life in America*.

Although a tanner by trade Billings was possessed by the Spirit of Music; and to the art, especially along the lines of choral composition and performance, he gave his best energies. His temperament was idealistic so far as his general approach to music was concerned, his vitality was enormous, and his contributions to church music both as composer and director were much greater in bulk and significance than those of any of his contemporaries or of those who immediately succeeded him. As a singer he does not seem to have shone; he had no gifts as an instrumentalist, for one arm was shorter than the other; but his administrative gifts were marked, and his anthems showed that he possessed a sort of histrionic sense leading to dramatic and emotionally effective performances. Tradition says nothing of his abilities as a tanner; whatever he earned that way may have been supplemented by money earned in teaching. Some of the qualities of mind and disposition that found outlet in his music are not inconsistent with business success. In 1774 he established a "Sacred Singing School" in Stoughton; this had about forty-eight pupils, all, I imagine, adults. This adventure of Billings led, in 1786, to the formation of the Stoughton Musical Society which carried on energetically for years and is still in existence. All this time (1770-1786) he was publishing music-books which we may believe met with a fair sale, *The New England Psalm-Singer* (1770), *The Singing Master's Assistant* (1778), *Music in Miniature* (1779), and *The Suffolk Harmony* (1786); at any rate they were saleable material for his pupils as well as for all other singing-teachers and their schools.

The style or format of the Colonial collections was generally oblong, and this format persisted for more than a hundred years. The pages were seven to eight inches wide, four to five inches high. Billings's *Music in Miniature* was an exception, being a very small book, upright, pages two and a half inches wide and six inches tall. The music of the early psalters in England was type-set, although later on music was engraved, but in the United States it was not until 1786 that the *Worcester Collection,* the first book printed in New England from music type, was issued.

According to O. G. Sonneck (op. cit.), the first reference to Billings appears in the *Boston Evening Post* in connection with the advertisement of a concert to be given on November 9, 1764;

tickets were to be had at "Mr. Billings's shop near the Post Office." As Billings was eighteen years old at this time he seems to have been a precocious business-man, but this is not inconsistent with his general character. Already he must have been at work on the *New England Psalm-Singer,* which was published only six years later. That Billings was a good deal of a man is shown by his close friendship with Samuel Adams, Harvard graduate, Governor, later, of Massachusetts, and one of the signers of the Declaration of Independence.

It was as late as 1787 that Billings's music was performed in public concerts in Boston, although Andrew Adgate of Philadelphia a year earlier had given prominence to two of his anthems, *The Rose of Sharon* and *Arise, arise thy light is come.* We can without difficulty imagine Billings to be on the way to success. Yet, Sonneck remarks,[61] in reference to a benefit concert for Billings arranged for December 21, 1790, in Stone Chapel (King's Chapel nowadays), "Billings, and this will cause surprise, was in rather reduced circumstances, for a correspondent in the *Columbia Centinel,* December 8, 1790, expressed his satisfaction 'in hearing that a number of benevolent characters are determined to bring forward a Concert of Sacred Music for the benefit of Mr. William Billings of this town, whose distress is real, and whose merit in that science is generally acknowledged.' " Sonneck goes on to say:

"If we remember that Billings, born in Boston in 1744, had still to live almost ten years until he died in 1800, we cannot but regret that the last years of this remarkable man should have been spent in poverty. Remarkable not only for his musical naiveté, enthusiasm, latent talent and amateurish utterances, but also for his appearance. If Billings, 'somewhat deformed, blind of one eye, one leg shorter than the other, one arm withered, and . . . given to the habit of continually taking snuff', attended the testimonial concert we may feel sure that Bostonians looked with pity and sympathy on this tanner-musician."[62]

A search for psalm- or hymn-tunes attributed to Billings yields the names of two hundred and sixty-three.[63]

---

[61] Op. cit., pp. 288-289.
[62] See Appendix E.
[63] See Appendix H.

Like the collections of the period the *New England Psalm-Singer* is oblong, and about 7¾ inches by 5½ inches; and numbers pages x —100 and index. One of the persons named to sell the book is Josiah Flagg[64] of whom O. G. Sonneck speaks with some appreciation in his *Early Concert Life in America*. In the preface an anonymous writer gives an "Essay on the Nature and Properties of Sound," not scientifically of the present day, but highly creditable to both Billings and the author. The Reverend Dr. Byles contributes a sixteen-line poem on Music; I quote six lines:

> "Down steers the Bass with grave Majestic Air
> And up the Treble mounts with shrill Career.
> With softer sounds in mild, Melodious Maze
> Warbling between, the Tenor gently plays:
> But if th'aspiring Alto join its force,
> See! like the Lark, it wings its towering course."

The Colonial writers were given to that sort of thing, the English composer and theorist, Tans'ur too, being an habitual rhymester. The frontispiece of the *New England Psalm-Singer* is an oval, 6½ inches by 5½ inches; a table is shown with seven men singing from books, they seem to be beating time as all conscientious Colonials were expected to do. (See also the *Psalm Singer's Amusement*). Around the oval is the music which Billings calls a canon, but which proved to be that simple canonic form, a round. The frontispiece was engraved by Paul Revere. Obviously the canon would be extremely monotonous, as it was formed on three chords and with a rhythmic figure repeated *ad nauseam*. Very plainly indeed William Billings was showing off.

"In order to have good music, in a company of forty people twenty of them should sing Bass. . . . Much caution should be used in singing a solo, in my opinion Two or Three at most are enough to sing it well. . . . In my opinion double D, viz. an octave below the Middle Line of the Bass, is the most commanding and Majestic of any sound in Nature. . . . I have read several Authors' Rules on Composition and find the strictest of them make some Exceptions, as thus, they say that two eighths or two fifths

---

[64] For an account of Josiah Flagg's book see Appendix K.

may not be taken together rising or falling, unless one be Major and the other Minor . . . for my own part as I don't think myself confin'd to any Rules for Composition laid down by any that went before me . . . I think it best for every Composer to be his own Carver."

And here is this quaint 'Advertisement': "The Author to his great loss having deferred the Publication of these sheets for Eighteen Months, to have them put upon American paper, hopes the delay will be pardoned; and the good ladies, Heads of the Families . . . will zealously endeavor to furnish the Paper Mills with all the fragments of Linnen they can possibly afford: Paper being the Vehicle of Literature, and Literature the Spring and Security of human Happiness."

One hundred psalm-tunes appear in the collection and several anthems of considerable length and of the usual harmonic ineptitude. Their titles are: *The Lord is King; As the Hart panteth; The Lord descended from above; Hear my Prayer; Blessed is he that considereth the Poor.* There are four 'fuguing' tunes. Billings is fond of writing into his tunes solo bits for the voices or a few bars of duet, or something of the sort; but these breaks in the four-voice procedure do not make a 'fuguing' tune.

All the copies of the collection I have seen are in poor condition, and Paul Revere's engraving does his memory no credit.

At this stage of his career Billings had probably not considered with any seriousness the problems involved in making the poetic meter and musical accent synchronize. This is strikingly demonstrated in his anthems. *As the Hart panteth* begins with a shocking disagreement between music and verbal rhythm; but on the other hand, the second phrase, *So panteth my soul after thee, O God* is perfectly declaimed. Billings's anthems are spotted thickly with these infelicities; his harmony is that of a musical but illiterate person; even the 'dumb' passages however can not entirely prevent us from realizing that there is a spirit confined working desperately to free itself.

THE SINGING MASTER'S ASSISTANT

The Singing Master's Assistant (1778-9-81) is, according to Metcalf,[65] Billings's most popular book. The collection is oblong

---

[65] Op. cit., p. 60.

in form, (plates 4 inches by 7 inches). In the Massachusetts Historical Society's Library it is bound with the *Psalm Singer's Amusement* and *The Suffolk Harmony*; these are all good copies. There are twenty-five tunes and several anthems; among the anthems is *I am the Rose of Sharon*, Billings's most popular piece in that form. In Sonneck's *Early Concert Life in America* there are several performances of it noted; it covers six pages, and a good choirmaster might make something of it. Oliver Ditson (Boston) and J. Fischer and Bro., (New York) have published editions of *I am the Rose of Sharon* and of some others of Billings's anthems.[66]

In *Dunstable*, a sort of elaborate hymn-tune (the words being, "as pants the hart"), Billings uses three notes of the same length and same pitch to "pants," thus making a literal panting. Careful examination of all Billings's anthems would doubtless discover other instances of this curious literalism. The titles of the anthems are: *By the Rivers of Babylon; Hear my Prayer; Is any afflicted?; I heard a great voice; I love the Lord; I am the Rose of Sharon; Sing ye merrily; The States, O Lord* (a patriotic anthem); *Was not the day?*

A few quotations from this rather lively collection may not be amiss. "A Prick of Perfection—dot side of a note—is not well named in my opinion, because a note may be perfect without it: a point of addition is the best name." A word that seemingly fascinates all the theory writers, English and American, from Sympson to the early eighteen hundreds, is 'sink':

"A flat sinks a Note half a tone lower than it was before . . . likewise flats are used to *drive Mi* from one place to another . . . sharps are used to *draw Mi* from one place to another."

In the moods of time Billings was most exact:

"In the slowest Mood, Adagio, 4 seconds of time to each bar, using a pendulum 39 and two tenths in. long for one crotchet; second mood, *largo,* pendulum to beat two in bar should be 7 ft. 4 in. long, in proportion of time to *Adagio* mood is 5 to 4."

As the years rolled along all the N. E. composers learned that tempo was a purely relative matter, and that it was modified by the various Italian terms used.

---

[66] *Centennial Collection*, shortened, Stoughton Musical Society; *The States, O Lord* (a patriotic anthem); *Was not the day?*

Billings has a good word for that detestable 'grace' known as Transition:

"The grace of transition is sliding; not jumping from one note to another; it is called a grace because it does its work gracefully."

In using the transition one fills in the space between notes by singing the intermediate tones![67]

On pages 16-17 he has a few brief rules for forming and carrying on a singing-school.

MUSIC IN MINIATURE

Music in Miniature (1779) gets its title from its tiny size; it has seventy-four tunes indexed, comprising (1) old tunes from his former books, (2) borrowed tunes in the style of the older psalmody, and (3) new tunes. The Boston Public Library has a copy.

The psalm-tunes in the collection include, so far as recognized, Billings's tunes only. The notes are very small and indistinct; one needs a reading-glass to study the work in any comfort.

PSALM SINGER'S AMUSEMENT

The English Singers who have made tours in the United States of late years have accustomed us to think of groups of people singing madrigals, glees, or part-songs seated around a table with music in front of them. In like manner the title page of the *Psalm Singer's Amusement* (1781)[68] shows us singers and instrumentalists at a table. In his 'advertisement,' Billings says:

"As this Book is not designed for Learners, I thought it not essential to write an Introduction; but would refer the young Beginner to my former Publication entitled *The Singing Master's Assistant*, which I have lately reprinted."

The *Psalm Singer's Amusement* is not large (it contains 104 pages; 15 tunes, 9 anthems), and the musical value of the whole, not striking; the usual infelicities and venturesomeness, the parallel fifths and octaves, the unhappy but well-meant progressions are what we now expect from this composer. The plates measure

---

[67] See Percy A. Scholes's *Oxford Companion to Music*, Oxford University Press, 1938, p. 570.
[68] See Appendix F. See Metcalf, op. cit.

4 inches by 7 inches. None of the tunes in this collection is found in *The Singing Master's Assistant*. Four 'fuguing' tunes are included. Billings frequently uses a style in which the voices enter in sequence: these are not proper 'fuguing' tunes, for in the 'fuguing' tune the voices must enter not only in sequence, but also on points of imitation. He has a flair for contrasts of all kinds, and chooses words that are dramatic and intense.

MODERN MUSIC

Modern Music, interesting for its title, is, however, of little illustrative value, and is Billings at medium strength. Of course in his day there would be no comment on 'modern', that is, modern music as it exists in the twentieth century. He does allude to such music in a passionate fit against 'Jargon', but the few measures he writes and prints as an example of 'Jargon' have no significance even as caricature; 'Jargon' is too infantile to be successful mimicry.

The plates are too small for a decent size of notes, the notes sounded simultaneously are not on the same vertical line from part to part, and since engraving and press work are poor, the music is very difficult to read.

The titles of anthems are: *Thou, O God; The Beauty of Israel; Blessed is he . . . ; And I saw; They that go down; Who is this?; Down steers the Bass* (Billings sang bass!); *Let every mortal ear attend; Vital Spark of heavenly Flame* (Pope).

THE SUFFOLK HARMONY

The Suffolk Harmony, with the same general style of the preceding collections, was published in Boston in 1786, had 56 pages, and was engraved. The titles of the anthems are: *Union; Lift up your Eyes; A funeral Anthem;* Easter Anthem, *The Lord is Risen;*[69] *Except the Lord build the House.* The edition of this work in the Massachusetts Historical Society has two folios of 8 pages each as appendices.

---

[69] See cut of frontispiece, *The New England Psalm-Singer.*

Finally came *The Continental Harmony* in 1794. This was printed typographically by Isaiah Thomas, a noted printer of the day; it was not, however, the first collection in New England to be printed from movable music-type, that distinction being reserved for the *Worcester Collection* (1786). There are two hundred pages, oblong 4½ inches by 7½ inches.

There is a long introduction of thirty-four pages corresponding to the older 'grounds' though not so named; twenty-two pages of the thirty-four are devoted to a colloquy between "Master" and "Scholar" on the rudiments of music; the respectful, not to say awesome, tone with which the Scholar addresses the Master approaches the ludicrous at times. (This induces the reflection that in America nowadays we are well over that sort of thing.)

I quote a few things from the colloquy. As to 'liningout' or as the Master calls it, 'reading between the lines': "Double bars in Psalm-Tunes are placed at the end of the lines for the benefit of the sight, to direct the performer where to stop, in congregations, where they keep up the absurd practice of reading between the lines, which is so destructive to harmony and is a work of so much time, that unless they have very good memories, they are apt to forget the tune, while the line is reading. I defy the greatest advocate for reading between the lines to produce one word of Scripture for it, and I will leave it to all judicious people, whether it is founded on reason; and certainly whatever is founded neither on reason nor religion, had better be omitted."

Scholar having apparently digested that long involved statement next asks, "Sir, I should be glad to know whether the grace of transition should ever be used in tuning thirds up and down."

Master replies: "Where the time of the notes will admit of it, I am very fond of the notes being graced by sounding the intermediate note, which serves as a stair for the performer to step up and down upon; but where the notes are but a half beat in length you must not strike the intermediate note."

In *Continental Harmony* details of notation are very badly attended to. Notes that should be sounded at the same moment should be on the same vertical line; if not so, related score reading is very difficult. There are seventeen anthems in *Continental*

Harmony. Taking any one at random something may be learned of Billings's method in composition and of his ability. In writing longer compositions than psalm-tunes he may not have had the idea that an anthem, for example, was simply a number of psalm-tunes, one after the other; but there is nothing in his anthems, looking at their structure, inconsistent with such an idea.

Analyzing *Universal Praise, Continental Harmony*, pp. 97-104, we note that it is made up of ten sections from ten to thirty-two measures in length, each section coming to a dead stop with the authentic cadence in C major; at the words 'roll the drum' there is a feeble attempt at realism, and there are one or two changes of time-signatures. As regards tonality, rhythmic effect and stoutness of structure they are much of a sameness.

When Billings and his followers attempted pieces where it was necessary to have some form in order to hold the music together, they always failed completely. And yet Billings and a few of the others had been endowed by nature with the melodic gift. Billings's basses are often free; they are efficient in the sense of contributing generously to the total effect.[70]

There are two interesting and important questions in regard to Billings as a musician that we may no longer evade; they ought to be asked and answered. (1) What knowledge did he have of the main stream of English psalmody as represented by Ravenscroft, John Playford and the seventeenth century music? (2) What influence did the English psalmody have upon his musical ideals?

The first question may be answered inferentially by taking note of the psalters and collections of psalm-tunes that circumstances indicate he probably knew at the date of the publication in 1770 of his first work, the *New England Psalm-Singer*. Ravenscroft's *Whole book of Psalmes* (1621) was then about one hundred and fifty years old; Billings may never have seen a copy. John Playford's work (1677), however, was the foundation of Reverend John Tufts's *Introduction to the Singing of Psalms*; the fifth edition (1726) must have been known to Billings, and it had a good collection of the English tunes, some of which he must have found to his taste. In 1766 when he was twenty, Billings must have seen copies of the irrepressible Daniel Bayley's *New and complete*

---

[70] See Appendix G.

Introduction to the Grounds and Rules of Music derived from *Walter* and *Tans'ur,* book two of which contained the substance of William Tans'ur's *Royal Melody.* Josiah Flagg of Boston had published a collection of the best psalm-tunes (1764),[71] containing Handel's sprightly march from *Richard III,* a tune that, if Billings ever had seen or heard it, would have given him inspiration for some of his liveliest work. Bayley had also reprinted in 1769 Tans'ur's *American Harmony or Universal Psalmodist.* We must not forget, either, that in 1758 and 1765 the supplement to *Tate & Brady's Psalter,* containing the music, had been printed in Boston. Since the ninth edition (with music) of *The Bay Psalm Book* had appeared in 1698, it is not unreasonable to think that Billings had seen it; but even if he had seen it he would have probably thought it crude in its two-part harmony and its solemn, reserved emotionalism. Giving these considerations a fair amount of weight can we doubt that Billings had been exposed to the influence of some of the good English music?

On the other hand it is the opinion of the *Musical Reporter* of January, 1841, (Boston Public Library), that Billings "had seen probably no work on the science of rules of harmony, except Tans'ur's *Grammar,* a meager and imperfect treatise." Tans'ur's *Grammar* ("Elements of Music or its Grammar or Ground-Work made easy"), if studied by Billings, would, I believe, have instructed him sufficiently to ensure an avoidance of his grosser errors, such as parallel fifths and octaves.

In the Preface to *Continental Harmony* (p. xxi, line 9 et seq.), he remarks: "Although I am not confined to rules prescribed by others yet I come as near as I possibly can to a set of rules which I have carved out for myself; but when fancy gets upon the wing she seems to despise all form, and scorns to be confined or limited by any formal prescriptions whatever. . . . The last parts are seldom as good as the first; for the second part is subservient to the first, the second must conform to the first and the third must conform to the first and second." A little reflection on these remarks by Billings warrants the assumption that he fitted his bass to his melody before writing the counter and tenor; and this would account for a good deal.

---

[71] See Appendix K.

58

I now come to the second important question in regard to Billings's ideals as a composer: What influence did the English psalmody have upon his music? The answer is, "None at all." Billings took his own way, and a wild way it was.

From the prefaces of his works we get an insight into Billings's character; he was by no means a timid, shrinking individual. Although in his music we are shown a musician of the tenderest sensibilities, he is at times, indeed often, a Boanerges of dramatic energy and imposes himself on you almost with violence. Some of his sayings support this view of his character:

"If you fall in after a rest in your part you must fall in with spirit, because that gives the Audience to understand another part is added, which perhaps they would not be sensible of if you struck in soft. In 'fuguing' music you must be very distinct and emphatic, not only in the tune but in the pronunciation; for if there happens to be a Number of voices in the Concert more than your own, they will swallow you up. Therefore in such a case I would recommend to you the resolution (though not the impudence) of a discarded actor who after he had been twice hissed off the stage, mounted again and with great assurance thundered out these words, 'I will be heard'."

Billings's magnificent self-confidence is also seen in the words written by himself, to the anthem, *Lamentation over Boston*. I omit portions:

"By the waters of Watertown we sat down and wept when we remembered thee, O Boston. . . . A voice was heard in Roxbury which echoed through the Continent weeping for Boston because of their danger. . . . If I forget Thee . . . then let my numbers cease to flow, then be my muse unkind, then let my tongue forget to move and ever be confined. Let horrid Jargon split the air and rive my nerves asunder, let hateful discord greet my ear as terrible as thunder, let harmony be banished hence and Consonance depart; let dissonnace erect her throne and reign within my heart."

This magniloquence, after all, has a languid strain of real feeling in it.

Billings was as ardent in helping his country during the Revolutionary War as he was in the composition of *Majesty*;[72] he wrote

---

[72] Page 64.

both words and music for the tune *Chester*,[73] which was the war song of the period, felicitously described by John Tasker Howard in *Our American Music* as the *"Over There"* of the conflict. Howard is wrong, however, in saying that Billings claimed God exclusively for New England: New Englanders had their own tribal deity who reigned forever, while others (doubtless referring to the British in particular) must get along as well as they could with their own. Billings's whole character is epitomised in the first stanza of *Chester*:

> "Let tyrants shake their iron rod
> And slav'ry clank her galling chains,
> We fear them not, we trust in God,
> New England's God forever reigns."

As a bold, vigorous tune *Chester* is good enough, but not much above the average of the Billings tunes. It has not the power of *Majesty* nor is it as tuneful as *Jordan,* which is easily the most spontaneously melodious of all his tunes; in fact it is more like a modern tune than any of the tunes of the period.

Although in the *Lamentation*—and this applies to all of Billings's work—nuances are missing, Billings contrives to make us feel what he wants done, and therefore changes in tempo and force and color suggest themselves. With that understanding an 'interpretation' of the *Lamentation* would be something like this: beginning *grave*; the frequent rests after 'wept' dramatize the situation; note the frequent G natural in the dominant chord of A minor; the bass passage *declamando* and faster; 'Forbid it, Lord', *Forte* and *energico*. 'A voice was heard,' *meno mosso*, patetico, and *a crescendo and dimuendo* on the word 'weeping' as it is passed about from voice to voice; phrase ends page. 'If I forget thee',—from here to the end beginning piano but increasing in speed and power, accumulating momentum through a savage earnestness, with a long *rallentando* in the final four bars. Interpreted in this way the anthem would, despite a sort of emotional and harmonic naiveté, convey a distinct impression of an active brain and an energetic, impulsive temperament expressing itself with emotional prodigality. If, however, we drop the role of a sym-

---

[73] Page 65.

pathetic interpreter and put on the cap and gown of the teacher of harmony we are bound to say that in *Lamentation* there is little to admire and much to regret. Any musician will recognize in the work (indeed in all of Billings's work and in the work of practically all of the early New England composers) an entire absence of all harmonic culture, the culture that was evident in Este, Ravenscroft, John Playford and by no means missing in Tans'ur and A. Williams.

As I have written above, Billings like all the Colonial composers who tried their hand at the anthem, can not give continuity to the musical line, nor does he have any idea of how to unify anything longer than a psalm tune; he relies entirely on a succession of more or less long phrases defined by strong cadences and separated by long rests. The usual errors made by music students in their first harmony lessons are common with Billings; but he does know how to space the words and he does, even if occasionally failing, synchronize the meter of the word and the rhythmic accent of the music.

An examination of Billings's music will show a crude experimentation with contrary motion, with a too ready yielding to the fascinations of passing-tones, with a lack of self-scrutiny that his exuberant temperament ought surely to have noted. Billings might have learned from Ravenscroft, Playford, from the old tunes heard in church, from the Reverend John Tufts's *Introduction* and from the Methodists' tunes in Wesley's *Foundery Tunebook* (1742) which, with some scandalously lively airs, had in it a number of the substantial tunes of the seventeenth century. It is quite possible that he had no power of self-criticism, nor of analytical power in general. It is also possible that his burning zeal for the American cause in the Revolutionary War had made him hate even the British psalmody. It is worth suggesting that the perfunctory performance, the lining out, the general dreariness of the psalmody that needed a fresh start, had tempted his impulsive nature.

One cannot devote any considerable time to a study of Billings's music without getting to both like the man and respect his music. He was a brilliant if headstrong and lovable wanderer from the straight and narrow way. Billings attained his majority in 1767 and his productive life was passed in the stirring times of the Revolutionary War. The Reverend Elias Mason, in a monograph, Albany (1869), writes, "Our forefathers were too busy to be musical. . . . God was their commander; the songs they sang were in the main addressed to him. . . . Even the Revolution did not produce any very creditable patriotic songs. The famous semi-sacred psalms of *Chester* and *Columbia* by William Billings were the camp songs of the day."

Having made up our minds that, to quote Sonneck, "Billings was a character, a personality more than a pioneer," we are still bound to give a more precise characterization of his genius, for genius he certainly had. That Billings was not a pioneer is proved by the fact that he had no following beyond the enthusiastic imitators who were aroused or stimulated by his contagious enthusiasm, his fertility, his musical independence of what to him must have seemed the senseless restrictions of the orthodox harmonist, and by his undoubted originality. What a cruel commentary on all that Billings wrote it is that, although artistic impulse was steady and very strong, there was neither the craftsman's culture nor the desire for it!

But even with that somewhat depressing admission of the futility of Billings's career as a composer of psalm-tunes and anthems is there not something more cheering to be said? Undoubtedly the music of the New England churches needed an infusion of geniality, an emotionalism of a different type, in their worship music, and this Billings supplied in his own compositions. He was no connecting link of one dispensation with another growing out of the old, but his vigorous temper and immense musical vitality kept the flame of emotional music alive, until something really better could come. To drop into a later aesthetic terminology, Billings was a romanticist.

The old adage, "Those that know nothing fear nothing," comes to mind as a comment on the music of the New England composers from 1770 to 1800; they had little musical knowledge, but their spirit was free, they wrote their tunes with a certain spontaneity and courage that we can not fail to perceive. How can we strike the balance between a contempt for their musical illiteracy and an unwarranted rebuke for their boldness? O. G. Sonneck[74] takes a sensible view of the matter. "Billings's tendencies and those of his rivals and imitators were working with tremendous force for the good of the future of choral music. In short it is easier to ridicule the technical shortcomings of these 'singing teachers' than to give them credit for their actual musical abilities and to ascertain their real historical importance."[75]

---

[74] Op. cit., pp. 310-311.
[75] For a list of 263 hymn-tunes by Billings see Appendix H.

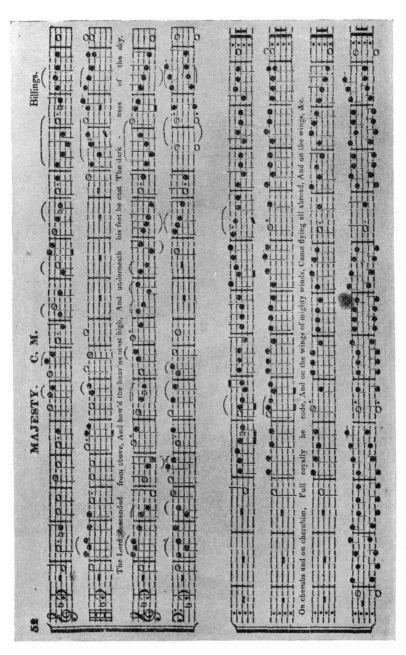

MAJESTY. C. M.

Billings.

The Lord descended from above, And bow'd the heav'ns most high, And underneath his feet he cast The dark - ness of the sky.

On cherubs and on cherubim, Full royally he rode, And on the wings of mighty winds, Came flying all abroad, And on the wings, &c.

(See pp. 50, 51, 57, 60, 75, 78.)

Majesty formally is a poor specimen of the "fuguing tune," yet the feeling and life are in it; there are some errors of harmony and of proof-reading. The words are the famous lines from the *Sternhold & Hopkins* version (1562), and to them is due much of the great popularity of the tune. An old aunt of mine, as late as the 1860's, used to impress the grandeur of *Majesty* on my young understanding.

64

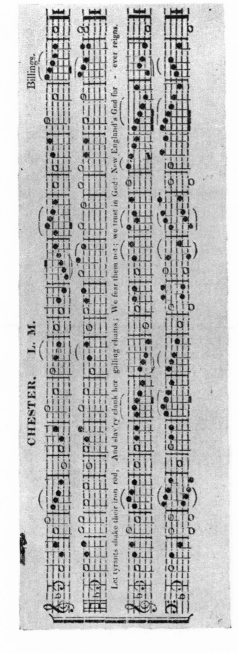

CHESTER. L. M.

Billings.

Let tyrants shake their iron rod, And slav'ry clank her galling chains; We fear them not; we trust in God: New England's God for - ever reigns.

(See pp. 51, 53.)

Quoting from John Tasker Howard.[76] "I learn that Billings's best known tune was *Chester*. It was popular in his own time, and was in wide use well into the nineteenth century. Always an enthusiast, he became one of the most fervent patriots during the War of the Revolution . . . . the song became the 'Over There' of the Revolution, with its fiery verses shouted by every soldier."

In both *Chester* and *Majesty* it will be noticed that Billings uses both a first and second bass part, usually in octaves; this ensures a strong foundation for the upper voices. Billings's basses were freer than those of other colonial composers.

[76] *Our American Music*, Thomas Y. Crowell Company, New York, 1930-1931.

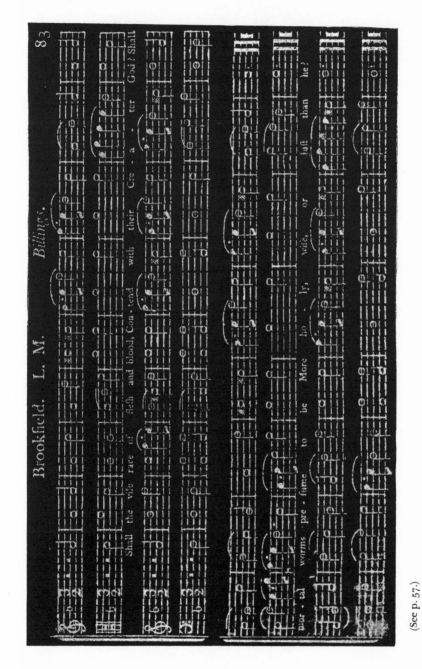

(See p. 57.)

Although *Brookfield* is one of Billings's poorest tunes, it seems better to accept Whittemore's selection of it as one of the choicer tunes of the period, than to substitute *Jordan* (to my mind a much finer tune than this one) for it. *The Columbian Repository* (1802 version) is used, though it is strange that Holyoke did not correct some of Billings's harmonic misadventures.

Africa. C. M. Billings.

105

(See p. 57.)

Africa is taken from *Village Harmony*, 10th edition, n.d. It appears also in Holyoke's *Columbian Repository*, 1802: It is strange that Holyoke, good musician that he was, should have passed the bare fifths, the parallel fifths and octaves of which there are several instances. This is an effective tune, with a slow, swinging rhythm.

67

CHAPTER TWELVE

The Music of the Billings Period (1746-1800)

Sonneck's study of American concert life[76] gives occasional references to singing-schools: "Undeniably the interest taken in music by the Yankees was keen, earnest and sincere, but outside of Boston it moved predominantly in the narrow channel of what we call psalmody, cultivated by the innumerable singing-schools and singing societies. Where we find in the newspapers one advertisement of a dancing-master or a musician anxious to teach the German Flute,[77] Harpsichord, Violin, etc., we run across a dozen advertisements of singing-teachers or of the publication of the psalm-tune collections (now so scarce) compiled by Stickney, Billings, Jocelyn, Read, Holyoke, Holden and others. However, sacred music did not predominate in the *provincial* cities of New England to the exclusion of secular matter . . . there of necessity must have existed an inherited and replenished store of secular music and consequently a vivid interest in secular music, at least six days in the week." Elsewhere Sonneck[78] refers to "the pioneer work done by the singing-schools since about 1720"; this date roughly coincides with the books by the Reverend John Tufts and the Reverend Thomas Walter, which were the earliest practical efforts devoted to instruction in singing and improvement in psalmody.

Professor Edward Bailey Birge[79] in giving an account of the development of interest in singing—particularly as regards singing of the psalms in worship—writes, "through advocacy of singing-

---

[76] Op. cit., p. 274.
[77] The flute traverso, not the flute à bec.
[78] Op. cit., p. 274.
[79] *History of Public School Music in the United States,* Oliver Ditson Co., Boston, 1928, Chapter One.

schools as a means of improving music in public worship they began to be established about 1720."

When William Billings was born (1746) the singing-schools had more than attained their majority, and his *New England Psalm-Singer* was timed to take advantage of the full tide of enthusiasm for singing 'by rote'. According to the summary given in Grove's *Dictionary of Music*,[80] up to 1800 (the date of Billings's death) there were 28 writers or compilers of psalmody books working in New England; 69 collections are associated through editorship or authorship with the 28. Sonneck speaks of the singing-books of the Billings period as scarce, but any search through the Lowell Mason Library at the Library of the School of Music, Yale University, the Massachusetts Historical Society's Library, the library of the Boston Public Library and the Congressional Library in Washington, D. C., will be well rewarded, as the present writer can testify.

Josiah Flagg in 1764 had published his 'Collection of the best psalm-tunes . . . approved by the best masters in Boston, New England.' In this he antedated Billings by six years.[81] Billings, however, may be considered the leader in the whole movement for better psalm-singing, his energy, fire and originality inspiring many of his contemporaries. It is true that the reaction against the somewhat bumptious egotism of the tanner-composer began to show itself as early as the last decade of the eighteenth century and the Billings tunes were tolerated as time went on only when 'corrected', to disappear from ordinary usage when those who had first sung them had died.

From collections like that of the Stoughton Musical Society (1878) or the *Billings and Holden Collection of Ancient Psalmody* (1836), made up of the old Billings period favorites unaltered, it is practicable to make a list of Billings contemporaries, choosing those whose music had passed the acid test of time. Such a list would reasonably include Daniel Belknap, William Billings, Lewis Edson, Jacob French, Oliver Holden, Samuel Holyoke, Jacob Kimball, Daniel Read, Timothy Swan. If one would care to narrow the list still more, one could take the testimony of the Rever-

---

[80] American Supplement, pp. 386-387 passim.
[81] Sonneck, op. cit., pp. 261-264. See also Appendix K.

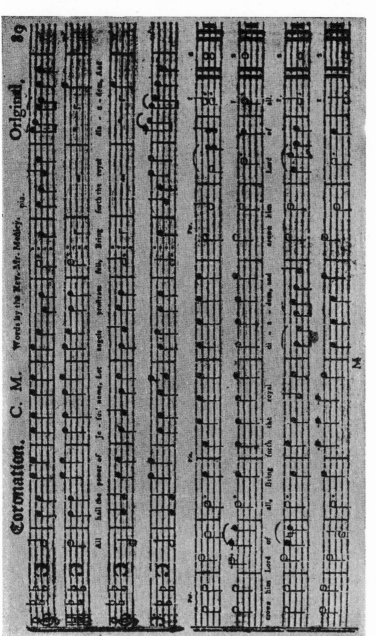

Coronation. C. M. Words by the Rev. Mr. Medley, pix. Original.

All hail the pow'r of Je-fus' name, Let angels proftrate falk, Bring forth the royal dia-dem, And

crown him Lord of all, Bring forth the royal di-a-dem, and crown him Lord of all.

(See pp. 57, 58, 127.)

Beginning with the top, the lines in the score stand for tenor (sung an octave lower than written), alto, treble, and bass. In American hymnals the key is always G. A few of the interesting things in this original may be pointed out. The 9th bass note gives the singer a choice. The 24th bass *f* (instead of *a flat*) persisted for a long time. The chord at the 25th bass note (mediant triad) is plainly meant for the dominant, i.e. with *e flat* (not *c*) in the tenor. The bold fifths between treble and alto, 17th and 18th notes ("him Lord") were corrected later. The four *g's* in the alto, "bring forth the roy-", are plainly misprints.

In a penciled note attached to a copy of the original edition in the Nutter Hymnic Library, Boston University School of Theology, it is stated that "the tune *Coronation* appeared in the first edition (1793). words by the Rev. Mr. Medley"; but in ink the "Rev. Mr. Medley" is deleted and "Edward Perronet" substituted.

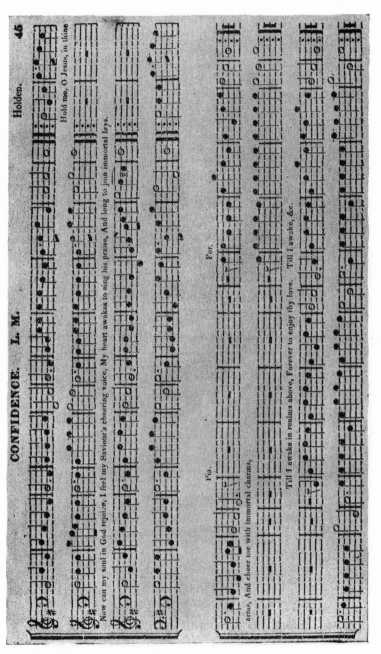

CONFIDENCE. L. M.

Holden.

45

(See p. 57.)

Confidence is from *Village Harmony*, 10th edition. This is one of the better Colonial tunes; the voice-leadings have a little adventuresomeness; there is effective modulation; there is continuity and a sense of climactic finish.

The resounding last six measures account for the effectiveness of the tune.

Beginning with the top line the score is tenor and alto (sung an octave lower), treble, and bass. The tenor and bass occasionally cross.

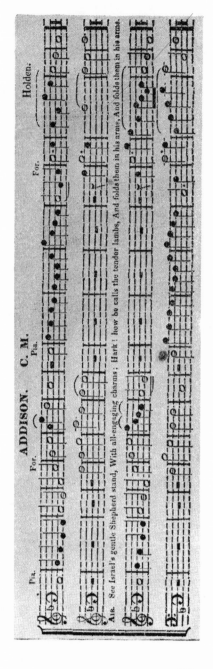

(See p. 57.)

Addison (Holden) from the Billings and Holden Collection.

See Israel's gentle shepherd stand,
   With all engaging charms;
Hark, how he calls the tender lambs
   And folds them in his arms.
     (Repeat last line.)

Holden had the endowment of a natural musician so far as a simple, intuitive melodic power is concerned; the simplicity of his harmony and the thirds and sixths accord well with the spirit of the words.

The score, reading from the top down, is for tenor (sounded an octave lower than written), the alto (sounded an octave lower), treble, bass.

72

end Thomas Whittemore (1800-1861), from 1820 until his death Universalist minister at Milford, Massachusetts, and of Cambridge, lawyer, prominent in business and political life, author of many religious books, who in 1836 named the following eight tunes as the best of those written in the Billings period, namely: *Coronation, Confidence,* and *Addison* by Holden; *Arnheim* by Holyoke; *Africa* and *Brookfield* by Billings; *Windham* and *Lisbon* by Read.[82]

It is strange that Whittemore did not mention *Majesty* by Billings, perhaps the most celebrated of all the Colonial tunes, as worthy of being included in a special list. So far as vital, emotional expression goes it might well have been added.

OLIVER HOLDEN[83]
(1765-1844)

If we seek information regarding the Colonial composers of psalm-tunes from the ordinary biographical sources we find that they were mostly men in humble life, not the sort of people that get into reference books.

This is not the case, however, with Holden, who was a man of affairs, a man about whom people wished information, and whose life was interesting enough to be recorded. He was a carpenter by trade, a book-seller, a minister of a somewhat unusual type, a justice of the peace; he kept a music store and taught music for many years. He was an ardent Free Mason, owned property in Charlestown, Massachusetts, Hillsboro, New Hampshire. He was born in Shirley, Massachusetts and was an active member of a congregation known locally as the "Puritan Church"; it was in the latter that he exercised the ministerial function, at least so far as preaching is concerned. Altogether, an interesting personality.[84]

Holden undoubtedly had a talent very little if at all inferior to that of Billings; his melodic invention was lyrical in feeling,

---

[82] A letter from Rev. Thomas Whittemore addressed to Lowell Mason under date of Oct. 27, 1836, accompanying a copy of *Songs of Zion* or the *Cambridge Collection,* 1836, and giving the above list of 8 tunes, is pasted in the cover of *Songs of Zion,* Lowell Mason Library, Yale University, School of Music.

[83] Grove, *Dictionary of Music,* American Supplement, gives 1834.

[84] F. J. Metcalf, op. cit., pp. 124-134, gives a detailed sketch to which the reader is referred.

whereas Billings in many cases had a robust tunefulness more instrumental than vocal; at times one is convinced that Billings knew John Wesley's *Foundery Tune-Book* (1742) and had been obsessed by the catchy rhythm of the Handel march there unblushingly set to sacred words.

Holden's collections in the order of publication were: *American Harmony* (1792); *Union Harmony* (1793); *Massachusetts Compiler* (1798), with Gram and Holyoke; *Modern Collection of Sacred Music* (1800), anon, but said by F. J. Metcalf (*American Writers and Compilers*) to be by Holden; *Plain Harmony* (1800), and *Charlestown Collection* (1825).

Judging by the number of tunes Holden published (27), he was Billings's nearest competitor for popularity. His principal claim on our attention is his authorship of *Coronation*, to the hymn, "All hail the power of Jesus' name."

Historically the tune *Coronation* has an importance justifying the paying of considerable attention to it. Out of the hundreds of tunes written in New England from 1770 to 1823 (the latter being the year Lowell Mason wrote his tune *Missionary Hymn*), *Coronation* is the only one now in general and approved used in the United States. Lowell Mason's tune bids fair to outlast *Coronation*, since it is included in the hymnals published for Anglicans, *Hymns Ancient and Modern* (765), *English Hymnal* (577) and in practically all of those used by the Nonconformists. In this respect *Coronation*, so far as I am aware, has never appeared in any British collection. Since 1797 Shrubsole's *Miles Lane*[85] has been the British tune for "All hail the pow'r of Jesus' name."

A good deal has happened to the tune since it left Holden's hands. It is interesting to see just what Holden wrote. Metcalf prints *Coronation* in its original form (1793).[86]

---

[85] Lightwood, op. cit., gives the best account of Perronet's hymn and the various English attempts to give it effective music, pp. 162-168. The tune *Miles Lane* is found in most English hymnals and in several American ones.

[86] Op. cit., page 126; the attribution is to the *American Harmony*, although the text gives *Union Harmony*, the latter being correct. *Village Harmony*, 10th edn., ca. 1813, supplies the version I use in this book; it conforms strictly to the *Union Harmony* version. While *Coronation* appeared in the great majority of collections from 1800 on, there were some strange omissions. It is not in Holyoke's *Columbian Repository*, nor in the first edn., 1802, of the *Bridgewater Collection* (although in the second edn., 1804), nor in the fifth edn. of the *Handel & Haydn Society Collection*, 1825, nor in the *Stoughton Collection*, 1829.

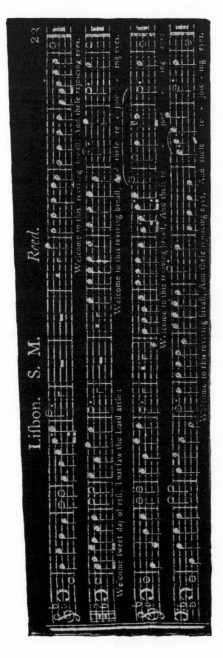

(See pp. 57, 60, 64.)

Welcome sweet day of rest
   That saw the Lord arise:
Welcome to this reviving breast,
   And these rejoicing eyes.

The bare fifth on "arise" is typical of the period. The sustained soprano, last four bars, with bass and tenor chattering along on "joi" makes a good effect; the Colonial choirs must have "eaten this up." The score beginning from the top is tenor (sounding an octave lower), alto, treble and bass.

75

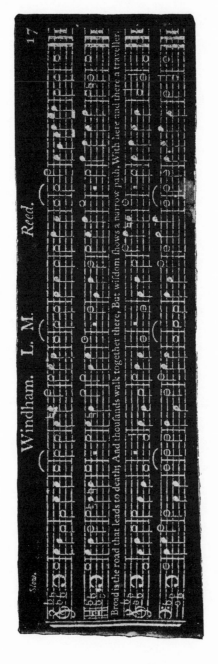

(See pp. 57, 60, 85.)

Windham is the classical example of the ignorance and shiftlessness of the New England composer in the eighteenth century. Like the tune *Wells*, by the English composer Israel Holdroyd, it was universally popular, and like *Wells*, it vexed and teased the American musical editors to give it its proper rhythmical form. One of the earliest editors to see that the time-signature ought really to be $^3/_2$ instead of $^4/_4$ or $^2/_2$ was he of *The Harmonist* (1837). The tune above is taken from the tenth edition of *The Village Harmony* (ca. 1806, Exeter, New Hampshire).

The words to which *Windham* was usually set are those printed with the music above.

The music on the whole was good enough to stand the march of time, and although modern editions are somewhat different from Holden's original, there was something on which to build. For the original edition with analysis, see p. 70.

Among American tunes Edson's tune *Lenox* is the only one whose lasting power is at all comparable to that of *Coronation*. The latter has a clear-cut form and vigorous rhythm, which fit it for the role it has played and will continue to play for a long time to come.

DANIEL READ

(1757-1836)

Daniel Read, like Oliver Holden, had a certain claim on public attention apart from his music. He was born in Rehoboth, Massachusetts, living later in Attleborough, but spending the most significant years of his life in New Haven, Connecticut. Grove's *Dictionary of Music*,[87] succinctly describes Read as "comb-maker and singing-teacher at New Haven." From the *Dictionary of American Biography* we learn that in New Haven Read entered into partnership with Amos Doolittle, an engraver; Doolittle seems to have been a man of culture and together they made and sold books and music. Sonneck[88] alludes to the musical club in New Haven, about 1786, called The Musical Society of Yale College; an elaborate advertisement in the New Haven *Connecticut Journal*, March 29, 1786, solicited subscriptions by Doolittle and Read for their *American Musical Magazine*, in which no piece, not previously examined by the said Musical Society of Yale College, was to be published. It would be interesting to know whether any budding composers of psalm-tunes took advantage of the stimulating opportunity. It appears that Read was prominent in the town, a member of the Governor's Guard, a stockholder of the bank, a director of the library.

Grove's *Dictionary of Music*[89] credits Read with: *American Singing Book* (1785-1794); *Musical Magazine* (1786); *Introduction to Psalmody* (1790); *Columbian Harmonist* (1793); *Ameri-*

---

[87] American Supplement.
[88] Op. cit., p. 311.
[89] American Supplement.

can *Musical Miscellany* (1798), *Northampton; New Haven Collection, Dedham* (1818). The Reverend Thomas Whittemore sponsored two of Read's tunes for inclusion in the best eight tunes of Colonial days. These are *Lisbon* and *Windham*. *Lisbon* is a 'fuguing' tune, which seems to indicate that Read was in sympathy with Billings as distinguished from Holden, who says in *Plain Psalmody* that he is opposed to 'fuguing' tunes. While *Lisbon* has a lively rhythm and a strong melody it is quite illiterate, if one judges it solely by the rules of harmony. The other tune, *Windham*, had a strange career; it followed *Majestey, Lisbon* and many other of the 'ancient tunes' in being altered and 'corrected' out of its primitive vigor, but it took until 1838 for a sympathetic editor (George Kingsley) to discover that its natural meter was triple and not duple. (See *Sacred Choir*, edited by George Kingsley.) *Windham* is usually sung to "Broad is the road that leads to death." It is worth noting that *Windham* is a minor tune. The proportion of minor to major tunes in the Colonial Psalmody was very large, amounting in some cases to forty per cent and over.[90] Modern tune-books do not favor minor tunes, although the recrudescence of the German choral has brought some minor examples of it into use, e.g. "O Sacred Head Surrounded," *Passion Chorale (Hymns Ancient and Modern*, 1924, No. 111); see also *Vater unser (English Hymnal*, 1933, No. 462). It is not unreasonable to predict a revival of interest in the old English minor tunes like *Burford, Bangor, Old 104*, or *Windsor*; or even to imagine that congregations at the present day might be taught to love minor tunes, provided the old style was followed, modern rhythm used, and a bit of modal flavor—not too much!—in evidence. Fourteen of Read's tunes, in their original form, are printed in the Stoughton Musical Society's *Centennial Collection* (1876).

What is the impression left on the mind after playing over these tunes? Largely that of a feeble musical mentality using a few fugal and rhythmical formulae over and over, but hardly sensing what is being done. Read usually has a long note at the beginning of the tune, which acts as a rallying point for a start; unfortunately it often prolongs an unaccented syllable and hence makes trouble.

---

[90] One must not forget the modal tunes of which *Martyrs* (Scottish) is a conspicuous example. See *English Hymnal*, 449.

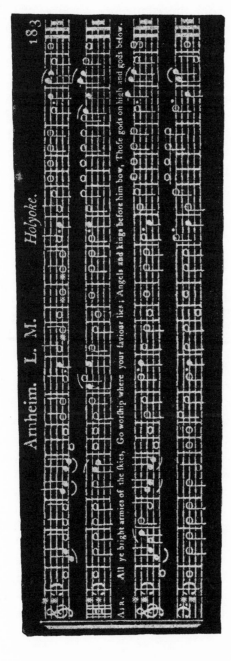

(See pp. 57, 62.)

Arnheim was written in 1778; the version used here was taken from Holyoke's own *Columbian Repository*, (1802):

> Now for a tune of lofty praise
> To great Jehovah's equal Son
> Awake my voice in heavenly lays
> Tell the loud wonders he hath done.

This tune was highly regarded by the Colonials, and it appears frequently in the collections. The hymn is grandiloquent and Holyoke played up to its emotionalism, the climax in the fourth phrase giving ample opportunity, in its high pitch, for brilliancy and power.

He uses, occasionally, the curious device, often found in the seventies and eighties of the eighteenth century, of holding the tenor and bass, through the rests in treble and alto, at the ends of middle phrases. He is fond of the 'fuguing' tune; four out of the fourteen tunes in the Stoughton *Centennial Collection* are of the type. Like most of the Colonial composers Read treats the leading-tone of the minor scale with scant courtesy, often adding the characteristic accidental (g sharp in A minor, for example) only at the last cadence. Bad proof-reading may often be responsible for the omission, or it may be a subconscious gesture towards modality, or may be simply that the Colonial composer liked that sort of thing: oftentimes the omission is effective.

SAMUEL HOLYOKE

(1762-1820)

Samuel Holyoke (A.B., Harvard, 1789), according to Sonneck,[91] was the founder of the Essex Musical Association, and director of their concerts; "performances were to be vocal and instrumental with 'bass viols, violins and flutes as instruments used at present'." He was a son of the Reverend Elizur Holyoke of Boxford, Massachusetts, and a busy singing-school teacher, his work lying not only in Boxford,[92] where his father was pastor for a long time, but also in the neighboring towns, Salem, Massachusetts, Exeter, New Hampshire, and so on. His general attitude towards music was that of the educated man, and he must be classed with those Colonial musicians who were looking for a new era in music that should eschew the extravagances of Billings and aim at harmonic correctness. His principal works are: *Harmonia Americana* (1791); *Massachusetts Compiler* (1795), with Hans Gram and Oliver Holden; *Columbian Repository of Sacred Harmony* (1802); *Christian Harmonist* (1804); and *The Instrumental Assistant* (1807).

Holyoke's *Columbian Repository* I judge to be the largest, most ambitious, of all the Colonial psalm-, hymn-, and tune-books. It had 734 tunes, occupying 472 pages, these including pages of *errata* and a list of subscribers; there are twenty-four pages in excellent style, of what was formerly referred to as "the grounds of

---

[91] Op. cit., p. 321.
[92] A small town near Salem.

music." The list of subscribers is suggestive of the range of Holyoke's friendships; the Essex Musical Association took 24 copies; Mr. A. March, bookseller of Newburyport, took 200; 3 students of Dartmouth College and the Musical Society took 6 copies amongst them; Benjamin Abbot, A.M., Preceptor of Phillips Academy, Exeter, took one; and Gardiner Spring, student at Yale College, took 12. It has been caustically remarked that no musician was ever known to buy anything that another musician had composed; I am glad to prove that false, since Mr. P. A. von Hagen, jun., Jacob Kimball, jun. Esq., Amos Blanchard, Jeremiah Ingalls, Abram Maxim, all of them professional musicians, subscribed. The format is oblong, eleven inches by nine, the music is type-set and the whole appearance of the work is handsome. The subscription list shows that 564 copies were taken in advance of publication: these, it has been stated, were sold for $3.00 each, or $1,692.00 in all. The expense of publication, however, must have been great. An examination of the book will make clear its fundamental weakness: 349 out of the total number of tunes had never before been printed, and there is seldom in connection with these 349 any attribution of authorship. We conclude that Holyoke himself had called upon his Muse to do the work. There were in addition to the 349, 332 tunes from the English psalmodies, and 53 American tunes. The work was, at this critical period of Colonial sacred music, loaded with useless material.

Holyoke was more of a musician than Billings, Read, or Holden; by that is meant that he had thought more about the management of the voices as regards variety and effect, having also due regard to the rules of harmony; he evidently saw that the 'rules' were precepts of advice for the benefit of the advisee. It follows, as in most cases where the brain and the emotions are both factors in a product, that sometimes Holyoke is more correct than pleasing, his tune *Woodrow* for example. Take Holyoke's tunes *Epping* or *Loudon* and you have him at his best. He is never as emotional as Billings, but much better schooled than any of the Colonials. The hymn-tunes forming the basis of these criticisms are *Arnheim, Epping, Hinsdale, Loudon, Mentz, Woodrow*. If, however, we look at Holyoke's longer pieces, for example his anthem, *"O praise the Lord"* (five pages long) we see how feeble is his grasp of any

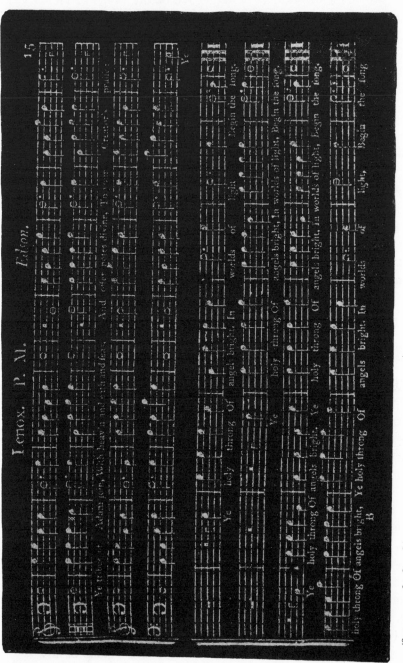

(See pp. 59, 64, 65, 78.)

Lenox appeared first in 1782 and has lasted longer than any of the 'fuguing tunes' of this period. As late as 1911 (28th edition of *In Excelsis*, The Century Company, N. Y.), it appeared in its fugal form with its errors corrected in accordance with contemporary taste; it has also found its way into *The Old Tunes*, edited by Dr. Dunstan, modern, n.d. with three changes in the tune and attributed to Russell (?) or Edson. The long first chord was a habit of Colonial composers. Several bare fifths will be noted. The words used were Charles Wesley's "Blow ye the trumpet blow" (1750).

form more complicated than the form of his beloved hymn-tune. While his tune *Loudon* holds together well and is effective music, the anthem is broken up into little scraps of music, separated from other scraps by rests; the effect of the whole is boring or laughable: one takes one's choice. Holyoke, however, was not without capacity and was headed properly: he would doubtless in time have developed along the larger forms. He seems to have been looked upon by some of his contemporaries as superior; for in the preface to the Boston *Handel and Haydn Society Collection* it is stated that he was exempted from the technical criticism directed to many of the composers of the period.

An instructive comparison of Holyoke and Holden in the manner of Plutarch might be made. Holyoke a bachelor; Holden married, the father of six children. Holyoke a university man, born in the intense and idealistic New England religious atmophere; Holden a practical man of affairs, a landowner, storekeeper, member of the Masonic fraternity, public-spirited, serving in the United States Navy (1782-1783). Holyoke's tunes forgotten; Holden's *Coronation* known pretty well over the world.

TIMOTHY SWAN
(1758-1842)

The Grove American Supplement attributes *Federal Harmony*, (Boston, 1785), *Songster's Assistant* (Suffield, 1800), *New England Harmony* (Northampton, 1801), and *Singster's Museum* (Northampton, 1803) to Swan. He was born in Worcester, Massachusetts, and died in Northfield, in the same State.

People of three score and ten now living must remember singing Swan's *China*[93] in church when children; the words to which it was usually sung began, "Why do we mourn departed friends?" The tune had a strange fascination for one little boy who used to hear his mother sing it, not realizing that it was a requiem for his sister, a darling girl baby. This was in the days of *Songs for the Sanctuary*. The same mother used to sing to the same little boy, "O Mother dear Jerusalem," she liking the tune and not knowing it was an old German drinking song. Hymn-tune books do not

---

[93] *China*, Swan's masterpiece, will long interest as a curio. See *The Story of the Hymns and Tunes*, Brown and Butterworth, American Tract Society, 1906.

nowadays introduce arrangements of drinking songs, although men who are wise in such things tell us that to the *Passion Choral* of J. S. Bach amorous words were sung long ago.

The Stoughton *Collection,* one of our valuable repositories of old music, has two tunes of Timothy Swan's in its edition of 1878, and notes that "his name stands emblazoned in glory in his *China* and *Poland." China* will be found in Metcalf, *American Compilers,* (p. 105). There are five other tunes by Swan in the *Billings & Holden Collection of Ancient Psalmody, Bristol, Ocean, Balloon, Lisbon* and *Rainbow.* There is little or no evidence in any of these tunes that Swan had any idea 'what it was all about'; he was the most original in his illiteracy of all the early American composers. He had evidently a good mind, but it was not a musical mind.

LEWIS EDSON
(1748-1820)

Lewis Edson, the composer of *Lenox,* the only 'fuguing' tune that has had place in a modern hymnal,[94] is not included in any of the usual biographical dictionaries; even Metcalf does not mention him; the American Supplement to Grove gives the dates of birth and death and connects him with Lewis & Thaddeus Seymour's *New York Selection of Sacred Music,* 1809 to 1816. The Stoughton Musical Society's *Centennial Collection,* appendix to its 1878 edition, gives his death as after 1824, but a manuscript note on the cover of a copy of Simeon Jocelyn's *Chorister's Companion,* places it two years earlier.

The manuscript comments on the copy of Jocelyn's collection make it easy to believe that the four tunes printed for the first time in the *Chorister's Companion*[95] (1782), *Lenox, Bridgewater, New Suffield, and Greenfield,* all by Edson, were the first music he had ever written. This will account for the (shall we say?) 'infelicities' of harmony and form disclosed in the original *Lenox.*[96]

---

[94] *In Excelsis,* edn. 1911.

[95] See *Chorister's Companion* in the Massachusetts Historical Society's library.

[96] Simeon Jocelyn (1746-1823) in his *Chorister's Companion* prints twenty-four tunes by William Billings; also two tunes *(Stafford, Shatford)* for the first time anywhere. The 1782 edition has eighty-five pages, sixty-four pages of tunes, oblong format, well printed on thick paper. The four tunes of Edson are fugal. *In Excelsis* adopts 1782 as the date of *Lenox.*

Edson was a blacksmith; he was born in Bridgewater, Massachusetts, and it seems that his people were Tories; since Edson was of more than fighting age in 1775 his politics could not have helped him to popularity. The family removed to the western part of the State, to Berkshire County, and there he found a name for *Lenox*. Further particulars gleaned are that his father was named Obed, and that Lewis married 'a Washburn' in 1770. He was director of music in several New York churches and died at his farm in Woodstock, Ulster County, New York.

DANIEL BELKNAP

(1771-1815)

Daniel Belknap, according to Metcalf (op. cit.), was farmer, mechanic and music teacher. He was born in Framingham, Massachusetts, and died in Pawtucket, Rhode Island. His collections are: *Harmonist's Companion* (1797), *Evangelical Harmony* (1800), *Middlesex Collection* (1802), *Village Compilation* (1806), *Middlesex Songster* (1809?). The Stoughton *Centennial Collection*[97] prints four of his tunes, *Blue Hill, Hampton, Holliston* (a town next door to Framingham), and *Lena. Village Compilation* had one hundred forty-seven tunes, fifty-three of which were Belknap's composition: from this it will be seen that he was a fruitful composer. Metcalf ends his interesting article on Belknap by saying: "His opportunities for acquiring a knowledge of music were limited. . . . His music became more or less popular for awhile, but it has not survived and is no longer sung." To which, let us add, "It's just as well."

JACOB KIMBALL, JR.[98]

(1761-1826)

We find copies of Kimball's tunes in the *Village Harmony*, tenth edition (1812?), namely *Ashby, Bradford, Brentwood, Byfield, Fairford, Funeral Anthem,* "I heard a great voice from heaven," *Harlem, Inconstancy, Invitation, Leicester, Plainfield, Topsfield* (his birthplace), *Tunbridge, Woburn, Yarmouth.* The

---

[97] 1878.
[98] Class of 1780, Harvard University.

1878 edition of the Stoughton *Collection* has *Falmouth* and *Middleton,* not in the *Village Harmony.*

A somewhat close examination of Kimball's tunes has developed some interesting ideas. It cannot be claimed for him that he had the natural emotional response to music that Billings and Holden, or even Read or Holyoke had, nor did there seem to be the same close relationship existing between the texts he selected for his musical settings and the music itself that was so marked in the case of Billings; but in some respects he shows an advance over any of the composers named: (a) he now and again uses some of the more modern chords—diminished seventh, the so-called German Sixth, and one or two of the chromatic chords in the key; (b) he has the knack of creating a feeling of unity by repetition with second endings; (c) his sense of rhythm and of rhythmic contrast is good. If these three faculties had rested on a spontaneous feeling for emotion in music, like that boiling resurgence we feel in Billings, he would probably have been a bigger man than the redoubtable Boston tanner. On the whole Kimball's attitude towards music is compounded of natural love and intellectual curiosity with the latter in command.

JACOB FRENCH

(1754-?)

Jacob French was born in Stoughton, Massachusetts. A brother, Edward, born in 1761 in Stoughton, died in Sharon in 1845 where he had always resided. In the account of the famous competition between the Stoughton Musical Society and the choir of the First Parish, Dorchester, an anthem of Jacob French, 'The Heavenly Vision,' was one of the two pieces sung by the victorious Stoughton contestants. The Stoughton Musical Society's collection, edition of 1878, gives the music of three anthems and four hymn-tunes by Jacob French, including 'The Heavenly Vision'; the words of this have to do with the Judgment Day, when "thousands of thousands and ten times thousands of thousands stood before the Lamb." The horrors of the Day of Wrath are depicted. The influence of William Billings is seen in the form of the anthem, which has seven phrases, all in the key of G major, and all ending in a full

86

authentic cadence. Nothing seems to be known of French's death or of his later history.

ABRAHAM MAXIM

(1773-1829)

Chronologically we may seem to be getting beyond the Colonial Psalmody of the Billings type, yet an examination of the collections made by Abraham Maxim and the tunes that he wrote will carry us back to the year 1770, the date of the appearance of William Billings's first book. Maxim's *Oriental Harmony* (1802) and his *Northern Harmony* (1808, second edition; fifth edition, 1819), exhibit much of the disregard for what, in view of the music of the ultra-modern composers of the twentieth century, may be called the "conventions of the seventeenth and eighteenth century harmony text books." In Maxim's case his five tunes, *Buckfield, Hallowell, Hartford, Portland,* and *Turner,* are in the 'fuguing' style, the imitative voices entering in either this order, bass, soprano, alto, tenor, or in this, bass, soprano, tenor, alto. He ingeniously offers an improvement on the Billings plan, namely to have a second theme entering in imitative sequence. Maxim's rhythmic feeling was strong, but seemingly confined to duple measure.

BARTHOLOMEW BROWN

(1772-1854)

For biographical details see Metcalf.[99] *The Billings and Holden Collection* has two tunes by Brown, *Tilden* and *Evelyn,* but Holyoke's *Columbian Repository* does not include any of his work. His chief claim to our attention is his connection with the Boston Handel and Haydn Society, as president at one time, and with the *Templi Carmina* or *Bridgewater Collection.* The *Bridgewater Collection* ran to twenty-seven editions and is easily one of the most important of all the early nineteenth century New England collections.

---

[99] Op. cit., pp. 150, 152; 168-171.

OLIVER SHAW

(1779-1848)

At the age of twenty-one Oliver Shaw became wholly blind. His natural musical endowment was considerable and his energy, great. He seems also to have had business ability and succeeded in building a fine connection in and about Providence, Rhode Island, as practical musician and music-teacher.[100]

Shaw was fortunate enough to have instruction from three musicians of European training, one of whom, Gottlieb Graupner, undoubtedly influenced Shaw to the good; for Shaw's compositions in technique and general substance are somewhat superior to all of the Colonial composers who had preceded him.[101]

ANDREW LAW

(1748-1821)

Andrew Law, dismissed by Sonneck[102] as "the melodist whose erratic career would be well worth a monograph," was born in Milford, Connecticut, was graduated from Brown University in 1775, received the A.M. three years later, traveled rather widely in New England and the Middle States as a teacher of music, was ordained a minister in 1787. After Milford, he resided in Cheshire, Preston, Newark, Philadelphia, and perhaps in other places, his work being in music and not in the ministry. He died in Cheshire.

Many of Law's collections, particularly his *Art of Singing* (in three parts, the first and third part published in 1801, in ordinary notation; the three parts in Law's new notation in 1805) are found profusely in libraries paying any attention to Colonial music-

---

[100] See F. J. Metcalf, op. cit., pp. 179-184, for an excellent account of Shaw. The Providence Public Library has considerable material, which supplements the music by Shaw and newspaper cuttings found in the Rhode Island Historical Society, Providence. On August 5, 1936, *The Pawtucket Times* (Pawtucket, R. I.) printed a special article on Shaw, with a copy of his *Trip to Pawtucket,* a piece for the piano.

[101] Shaw's *The Columbian Sacred Harmonist or Collection of Grammatical Music* (excellent copy), 1808, pp. 126, Library of Massachusetts Historical Society; *Melodia Sacra or Providence Collection of Sacred Music,* 1819, pp. 152, Yale University Library; *The Providence Selection* 1815, pp. 128, excellent copy in Providence Public Library, Providence, R. I.

[102] Op. cit., p. 123, foot-note. Also see MS letters about Law in Boston Public Library,** M. 317.5

books. Law's interest in music was the interest of a cultivated and educated man in a subject out of which he had pleasure; he also desired to influence music-lovers and would-be executants towards a realization of music as art.

A modification of his notational invention is in use at the present time in the South and West.[103]

---

[103] See Appendix I.

CHAPTER THIRTEEN

Harmonic Inheritance of the Colonial Composers

One does not need to be in the least clever to detect in the Colonial psalmody violations of the simplest rules of harmony and part-writing as we understand those matters today. In the interests of a fair and exact criticism, however, we may profitably ask if there ever was any body of harmonic practice from which the Colonial composers might have derived instruction; also, was this accessible to them? The answer to the first question is, yes; to the second, yes, but only indirectly.

That is to say, if we examine the music of Goudimel, Bourgeois, Clément Jannequin and others of the sixteenth century we can discern the harmonic practices of the period with absolute clearness.[104] Broadly speaking, the work of Este and the *Day Psalter* is in line with that of the *Calvin Psalter* of 1562; this filters down through *Ravenscroft* (1621), the *Scottish Psalter* of 1635, *Playford* (1677), to be reproduced (with additions or ornamentations of the harmonic structure) by men like Christopher Simpson (d. 1669), Aaron Williams (1731-1776), William Tans'ur (1700-1783), and others, bringing us down to the Colonial period. The analysis of the teachings of Christopher Simpson and William Tans'ur strikingly support the statement that a corpus of careful and logical practice by composers from the sixteenth century to the issuance of Billings's first book was known to musicians.

But was this corpus of musical practice in any real or practical sense known to the New England composers? No really satisfactory reply can be given. It is easy to demonstrate the existence of good music and sound theoretical works on the composer's business in existence and in circulation from 1620 on; but did Billings for

---

[104] Douen, op. cit., vol. 2. See also Appendix M.

example ever see a copy of *Ravenscroft* or *Playford* or of *The Bay Psalm Book?* No evidence seems ready; the argument must be all on an *a priori* basis. I have gone into this matter also in the chapter on Billings, to which the reader is referred.

CHRISTOPHER SIMPSON

(d. 1669)

Christopher Simpson's, *A Compendium or Introduction to Practical Music,* published in 1667, but reprinted in many editions after his death in 1669, was the work of a good musician and we may take the book as fairly representing professional standards in general theory and composition. I am quoting from the fifth edition of 1714; there were editions as late as 1770, the date of William Billings's first work, *"The New England Psalm-Singer."* Grove's *Dictionary of Music and Musicians* speaks of Simpson as "a distinguished 17th-century viola di gamba player famous in his day as an executant and theoretic musician."

In Simpson's work just mentioned he describes the system founded on the solmization of the major scale as *fa-sol-la-fa-sol-la-mi,* clinching the matter (p. 4) by the statement that

> *"mi-fa-sol-la* taken in their significancy are necessary assistants to the right tuning of the degrees of sound."[105]

Pages 10 to 18 in Simpson's book deal with the ancient moods of time and measures of notes; those still used in Billings's day and later are semi-breve, minum (note the spelling) or minim, crotchet, quaver, semiquaver and demi-semiquaver. The dot at the side of a note is called a 'prick,' a dotted crotchet is a 'pricked' crotchet. Syncope or syncopation is referred to as 'driving a note', an excellent characterization. Triple meter or time is 'tripla.'

The second part of Simpson's book is "The principles of composition." What we now call harmony, he calls counterpoint. This is also the word used in the treatises on music for the harmonizations of a bass or melody, note against note. "In reference to Composition in Counterpoint," he says, "I must propose to you the *Bass* as the Ground-work or Foundation upon which all musical

---

[105] See Solmization, Appendix N.

91

Composition is to be erected." Here he seems to imply that the first step in composing music is to invent a bass, the melody (if there be one) to come second in point of time. Definitions of intervals, concords, discords (the fourth classed as a discord) follow. Although Simpson allows repeated perfect 5ths and 8ves, parallel or consecutive perfect 5ths and 8ves are forbidden (p. 32). Covered 5ths and 8ves are all right if the upper part moves one degree only (p. 33). Minor tunes are called flat, and major tunes, sharp. On page 37 he tells how to frame a Bass; and on page 38 explains the method of joining a Treble to a Bass; he confines himself, in adding notes to form Tenor and Alto to the Bass, to a 3rd, 5th, 6th or 8th from the Bass.

I cannot resist quoting Simpson (pp. 45-46) in passages showing that, with a notable exception, the harmonic resources of the period were thought to be exhausted by using triads in root position or in first inversion; root position was indicated by the 3rd, 5th, and 8th from the Bass; first inversion by 3rds, 6ths, and 8ths, with a further provision, that when the 6th from the Bass was taken the 5th from the Bass could not be used, and when the 5th from the Bass was taken the 6th could not be used. Simpson, however, is by no means inclined to let the matter rest there, and points out that Thomas Morley in his *Introduction to Musick* uses a chord with both a 5th (a diminished 5th) and 6th, this proving to be the first inversion of the supertonic seventh in minor. Simpson gets the conjunction of 5th and 6th in the first inversion of the dominant seventh chord in the minor.[106]

Some sensible rules for good voice-leading merge into a discussion of 'transition' which is nothing more than filling in the spaces of a tune or melody with passing tones. The New England composers followed their English brethren with great zeal and smeared their harmonies by the excessive use of 'transitions.' Simpson closes his second book or part by treating of 5, 6, 7 parts and 8 parts with double basses (see Simpson pp. 53-60). Simpson's third book is on discords, treating of discords, false relation (Relation Inharmonical), the diatonic, chromatic, and enharmonic scales, with

---

[106] Simpson says (p. 48), "thus you see how a 5th and 6th may be used at once; in any other way than these I have mentioned I do not conceive how they can blend together in Counterpoint."

a bit of speculation on what we would characterize as acoustical rudiments, etc. There are many musical illustrations and the whole is distinguished by clearness of statement and the wisdom of the practical musician.

WILLIAM TANS'UR

(c. 1706-83)

Tans'ur's first work[107] was *A Compleat Melody, or the Harmony of Sion* (1724); it had an active existence in England as late as 1766 and was influential in America. The book was published twenty-two years before Billings was born, and it is not unreasonable to assume that by the time Billings was twenty-four and had published *The New England Psalm-Singer,* he had seen Tans'ur's successful work. Whether Billings was moved by Tans'ur's book or profited by studying it we have no way of knowing. In the chapter on William Billings I have discussed the matter at some length. Tans'ur published several works on the elements of music, harmony, counterpoint, etc.; one of these, usually referred to as a 'grammar of music,'[108] came out in 1746, the year of Billings's birth and apparently was successful. Daniel Bayley of Newburyport used both Tans'ur and A. Williams in his reprints of English material (c.1750-1770) and there need be little question that Billings could have had access to this 'Grammar' by Tans'ur if he had so wished.

Book I treats of the gamut, clefs, kinds of notes, the graces or ornaments, vocal exercises ("tuning the voice"), time, keys, solmization (the practice of which Tans'ur strongly recommended), intervals. Book II is explained in rhyme:

> *The Organ's* Structure's *here set forth in View*
> *The* Viol, Hautboy, Flute, *and* Scales *most new:*
> *How* Peals *are tun'd and how the* Chimes *do play:*
> *And chearful* Songs *to drive dull* Cares *away.*

---

[107] See Lightwood, op. cit., pp. 110-112; *British Musical Biography,* J. D. Brown and S. S. Stratton, Birmingham, 1897.

[108] A/New Musical GRAMMAR,/and/DICTIONARY/or/A General INTRODUCTION/to the whole/ART OF MUSICK. In four books, third edition with large additions, by William Tans'ur, Senior. London, 1756; seventh edition, 1829, pp. xvi-176.

Book III treats of elementary acoustics and the ratios of vibration of the common intervals; twenty pages are used (with copious examples) to "the approved rules of composition." The illustrations are all in two voices only (treble and bass), and the instruction perfectly sound; Tans'ur forbids consecutive unisons or octaves, consecutive fifths, covered fifths and octaves by parallel motion, two major thirds in succession. Discords are recommended "when orderly taken," also by suspension; general rules for composition in four parts, with one example; and for composition in "5, 6, 7, or 8 musical parts;" canons of various kinds are touched upon briefly with two illustrations. The text is simple and creditable to Tans'ur's musicianship. Billings would have profited by the study of this book III.

Book IV is a musical dictionary.[109]

In the beginning of this chapter two questions were asked: (1) Was there a body of European (and particularly English) musical practice from which the New England composers from 1750 to 1790 might have derived instruction and technical inspiration? and (2) If there were such opportunities were they accessible?[110]

The first question, in the light of the preceding pages, was answered, with some positiveness, yes; the second question, yes, but with a certain reserve. A third question now obtrudes itself, (3) Did the Colonial composers avail themselves freely of these chances? At first blush one is inclined to say no. One thing is true, namely we have evidence (though not before 1795) that sensitiveness to the technical badness of their music did not show itself until the appearance of the *Massachusetts Compiler* (1795). By this time the influx of musicians from Europe had gone on and their effect on musical taste in America had become marked.

---

[109] A musician studying the history of New England psalmody, with ample time and an income sufficient for the purchase of the requisite books and for travel to libraries in the U. S. and abroad, would do well to make a brochure on Tans'ur; he was reprinted freely in America. Sonneck did not have a good opinion of Tans'ur's musicianship, but I believed that Sonneck was misinformed. Grove's *Dictionary of Music and Musicians*, article "Tans'ur," gives a full column to him, and states that "*A new musical grammar* is, for its time, an excellent treatise, and at the present day contains much of antiquarian interest."

[110] See Chapter XI for previous discussions on this matter.

CHAPTER FOURTEEN

The 'Fuguing' Tune

Although the Colonial composers have had to bear the weight of
the displeasure aroused by the 'fuguing' tune, we find that the English were not averse to using them. Lightwood alludes to this in his
Hymn-tunes and Their Story (p. 96); and John Arnold in *The
Compleat Psalmist* (1751) refers to "these new-fashioned fuguing
tunes."[111]

We learn that tunes in what were called 'Rapports' or 'Reports'
made their first appearance in the 1635 edition of the *Scottish Metrical Psalter*, although two of the eight there presented appear in
the Aberdeen edition of 1633. Fugal imitation was the leading device of seventeenth century music, and the 'Rapport' applied this
in a tentative way to psalm-tunes. The author of the preface to the
1635 edition of the *Scottish Metrical Psalter* says that the "Reports
are given for the further delight of qualified persons in the same art
(music); the probability is that they were sung by the more cultivated congregations in town."

A somewhat different account[112] of the 'Report' is given in the
Manual of Church Praise: "The psalm-tunes in 'Reports' of the
1635 Psalter were really short motets, in which the melody of some
proper tune (that is, a tune closely associated with a metrical psalm
by priority of use) was in each case used as a *cantus firmus*, the

---

[111] The 'fuguing' tune as written by the New England composers in William Billings's
day was only a pitiful imitation of that part of the fugue known as the 'exposition'; the
'exposition' was simply the entrance of all the parts or voices in turn at the beginning
of the fugue. Each voice sang the subject or the answer in its turn. In the Billings
'fuguing' tune, on the other hand, the successive entries of the voices took place at
the latter part of the tune, and the successive entries imitated the subject only
rhythmically.

If a person at all conversant with the early history of New England were asked to
name a 'fuguing' tune, it is probable that *Majesty* would be cited, but a brief examination of the music (page 64) will show that it does not qualify for the name.
The *Scottish Metrical Psalter* (1635) has eight psalms in 'Reports', only two of which
bear any resemblance to a fugal exposition.

[112] Published by the Church of Scotland Committee on Publications, 1932; see p. 47.

choristers (choir) being left to fit the words to the music, a feat re-
quiring a skill which only trained singers could achieve."[113] The
voices carrying the tenor (or church tune) would have the simple
task of singing the words of the psalm in regular sequence—Psalm
CXXXVII in 'Reports'—to the words:

> When as wee sate in Babylon
>   the rivers roundabout,
> And in remembrance of Syon
>   the tears for grief brast out,
> We' hanged our harps and instruments
>   the willow trees upon:
> For in that place men for their use
>   had planted many one.

In the Livingston reprint of the 1635 *Scottish Metrical Psalter*
there are no words with the music of the 'Reports'; but in Sir
Richard Terry's edition of the same work he has filled in the words
completely for all the four parts.

Aberfeldy in 'Reports,' from the *Scottish Psalter* (Aberdeen), of
1633, will be found interesting as more modern or rather less
archaic in style. It is found in the *Scottish Psalter*, Humphrey Milford, Oxford University Press, 1929, No. 191.

It may be added, in regard to the American fugal or 'fuguing'
tune, that the fugal or imitative section does not come until the
second part. The majority of the composers had little initiative in
the order of the entering of the parts, taking them often in sequence of Bass, Treble, Counter, and Tenor. Or, in the score of
the first Billings tunes the order is Bass, Tenor, Counter, Treble.

In this connection a letter from James Lightwood, author of
Hymn-tunes and Their Story, is of value:

> " 'Fugal' tunes seem to be confined to America and to tunes in 'Re-
> ports' in early Scotch Psalmody. They do not belong to English
> Psalmody, certainly not to 18th Century Methodist Psalmody. The
> only Methodist Tune Books of the 18th century are:
>> 1742 *The Foundery Tune Book*

1761 *Select Hymns with Tunes* Annext.	⎫ The Music
1765 *Select Hymns* 2nd edition	⎬ Selection is called
1770 *Select Hymns* 3rd edition	⎭ Sacred Melody

---

[113] See pp. 8-24 in *The Scottish Psalter* (1635), R. R. Terry, 1935.

1780 *Sacred Harmony* (large edition)
1789[114] *Sacred Harmony* (thin edition)

There were two later editions.
Other books in use amongst Methodist bodies were:

1746 Lampe's *Hymn on the Great Festival*
1754 *The Divine Musical Miscellany*
1757 *Harmonia Sacra* (printed for Thomas Butts)

The popularity of singing amongst the Methodists led various editors
to bring out collections of tunes for their use, but these are in no sense
authoritative. A notable feature of some of the tunes from 1761 was a
'Hallelujah' refrain, but in no instance is there any attempt at a 'fugal
tune' (assuming that some form of imitation is meant) nor have I
come across examples in other books I have examined."[115]

So far as the New England composers were concerned their
'fuguing' tunes were simply so many awkward bows and scrapes
to the fugue itself. To paraphrase W. S. Gilbert:

It is very ev-i-dent
Their in-ten-tions were well meant.

Billings thought well of the 'fuguing' tune and gives an eloquent
description of its emotional effect; he says: "It has more than
twenty times the power of the old slow tunes; each part straining
for mastery and victory. The audience, entertained and delighted,
their minds surprisingly agitated and extremely fluctuated, sometimes declaring for one part and sometimes for another. Now the
solemn bass demands their attention; next the manly tenor, now
the volatile treble. Now here, now there, now here again; rush on,
you sons of harmony." As late as 1824 the *Musical Cabinet* or *New
Haven Collection* had 11 'fuguing' tunes in its 141 pages. The
Stoughton Musical Society's *Centennial Collection* reprinted 58
of the old 'fuguing' tunes in its first 67 pages.

But the 'fuguing' tune was by no means universally approved;
in 1833 The *Methodist Harmonist* records its "cordial approbation
of that clause in our discipline which disapproves of fugue tunes".

---

[114] Not 1781 as given in "Hymn-tunes and Their Story."
[115] See Appendix N.

97

If we date the death of the fugue tunes from this condemnation, and its birth from the *Scottish Metrical Psalter* of 1635, it had a life of two hundred years, although *Songs of the Sanctuary* (1873), from which I sang when a boy, had *Lenox* in its 'fuguing' form.

In 1807 Elias Mann prefaced his *Massachusetts Collection of Sacred Harmony* by fulminating against the iniquity of 'fuguing' tunes: "In this collection will be found none of those wild fugues, and rapid and confused movements which have so long been the disgrace of congregational psalmody and the contempt of the judicious amateur." Almost at that very moment, however, Abijah Forbush included 26 tunes in the fugal style out of a total of 95 tunes in his *Psalmist's Assistant* (1806).

Harriet Beecher Stowe, in her *Poganuc People* (1879) gives a spirited account of a suppositious singing of Billings's famous tune, *Majesty,* time about 1820. She writes:

"and as there is a time and place for all things in this great world of ours, so there was in its time and day a place and a time for Puritan music. If there were pathos and power and solemn splendour in the rhythmic movements of the churchly chants, there was a grand, wild freedom, an energy of motion in the old 'fuguing' tunes of that day that well expressed the heart of a people courageous in combat and unshaken in endurance. The Church Chant is like the measured motion of the mighty sea in calm weather but those old 'fuguing' tunes were like that same ocean aroused by stormy winds, when deep calleth unto deep in tempestuous confusion, out of which at last is evolved union and harmony. It was a music suggestive of the strife, commotion, the battle-cries of a transition period of society, struggling onward towards dimly seen ideals of peace and order. Whatever the trained musician might say of such a tune as old *Majesty,* no person of imagination and sensibility could hear it well rendered by a large choir without deep emotion, and when back and forth from every side of the church came the different parts shouting—

> On cherubim and seraphim
> Full royally he rode,
> And on the wings of mighty winds
> Came flying all abroad.

there went a stir and thrill through many a stern and hard nature, until the tempest cleared off in the words—

He sat serene upon the floods
Their fury to restrain,
And he as Sovereign Lord and King
Forevermore shall reign.

And when the Doctor rose to his sermon the music had done its work upon his audience, in exalting their mood to listen with sympathetic ears to whatever he might have to say."

CHAPTER FIFTEEN

The Singing School

A brief recapitulation of the musical history of New England for the first hundred years may help us to understand the movement for a better psalmody in 1720.

The Colonists brought over with them their memories of the 'old' psalter which they had used during their years in England preceding the exile to Holland; we have no means of knowing how much that experience meant to them, but those who were musical and fond of singing doubtless took to Holland with them some of the noble tunes that were used in church.

The Colonists also had the *Ainsworth Psalter,* on the passage over and afterward in Plymouth, New England, for thirty or forty years; the tunes were considered rather hard to sing, and *The Bay Psalm Book,* ninth edition, with tunes in treble and bass (1698), proved an agreeable change from Ainsworth. Of course *Ravenscroft* was accessible from 1621,[116] but the tunes were in four parts and even a modern choir would have difficulty in accustoming itself to the occasional modal harmonies, the queer false-relations and the strange modulations, relics of the old musical dispensation.

John Playford's *Whole Book of Psalmes* in three parts (1677) was destined to have a salutary influence for a hundred years on psalmody in general, but the first direct help for the Colonials was gained through the medium of the Reverend Tufts's *Introduction to the Singing of Psalm Tunes,* in the early seventeen hundreds; the Reverend Thomas Walter's *Grounds and Rules* was also at hand and the two together inspirited the singers and stimulated their ambition. Both the Tufts and Walter collections were used largely in the new movement for singing 'by rule' and for doing away with 'lining-out'. So soon as the singing schools got fairly

---

[116] Governor John Endicott's well preserved copy of Ravenscroft is in the library of the Massachusetts Historical Society.

under way and the need for more printed music and better instruction in the 'grounds' became plain, collections appeared from nearly every quarter of New England, written or compiled by the men who had organized the singing schools.

Professor Waldo Selden Pratt[117] lists nearly three hundred seventy-five titles of about two hundred compilers. The period included is from 1620 to about 1860. Two hundred fifty of the titles are dated before 1820. The singing-school teacher was, under the circumstances, an itinerant seller of music books, for scholars must have the printed 'grounds' with an abundance of good and attractive music for practice and social enjoyment. A successful teacher would have little or no difficulty in getting a class year after year, but the class would need a variety of study-material, and this would result in the compiling of a new collection for a second and the succeeding season. There is little wonder that in the one hundred years from Tufts's *Introduction,* two hundred fifty collections for singing schools (a large proportion of them in New England) had been written and used in the Eastern States.

Professor Waldo Selden Pratt states that:

"popular classes for teaching the rudiments of music and practicing hymn-tunes arose in New England before 1750 in consequence of the movement to introduce singing by note in the churches.[118]

Sonneck considers that the singing schools began their pioneer work as early as 1720:

"The several choirs of Boston undoubtedly profited by the efforts of the singing schools to prepare young and old for a better understanding and a better rendition of the hymns, psalms and anthems used in the churches. That both in the singing schools and church choirs excerpts of Handel's works were studied with enthusiasm may be taken for granted, but neither William Billings nor his rival psalmodists seem to have possessed the necessary energy to bend opportunities towards the more systematic and artistic study, not only of sacred cantatas, but also of oratorios."[119]

Not forgetting the fact that the Scottish 'Sang Schules' antedated the New England singing schools by two centuries, an in-

---

[117] The American Supplement to Grove's *Dictionary of Music and Musicians,* edited by Pratt, article "Tune-Books."
[118] Op. cit. article "Singing Schools".
[119] *Early Concert Life in America,* p. 274.

teresting parallel or parallels might be drawn between them; each had for a motivating idea the improvement of the service of worship through bettering the performance of worship-music.

The singing school was important socially; it also developed a new profession, that of the music teacher, whose income was supplemented by the sale of the collections published from 1714 to 1800. The history of the American singing school[120] demonstrates its social as well as musical value.

After finding the sixteenth century editions of the Day or Ainsworth psalters typographically printed, the student will probably be surprised to note that the Colonial music books were engraved. Paul Revere was one of the engravers of music at the time of the Revolutionary War. The engraving done by him on the copy of the *New England Psalm-Singer* (Billings) in the library of the Massachusetts Historical Society will not enhance his general reputation, although it will vastly increase the value of the book to collectors.[121] The note-heads, sharps, flats, naturals, are hand-engraved, the five-line staves ruled by hand; consequently the appearance of the music is not better than that of an ordinarily good manuscript. The letter-press is close and at times nearly illegible. The Library's copy is completed by four photostats; the covers are broken; the pages are smooched and here and there illegible.

The copy in the Boston Public Library lacks pages 97-108 and was printed from damaged plates. (We must not forget that it was printed in 1770.) The score, reading from the bottom upward, is: bass (F clef), tenor (solreut or G clef), counter (C clef on third line), treble (solreut or G clef). The tenor part in treble clef when sung by men, sounded an octave lower than written; when sung by women, sounded at written pitch.

---

[120] E. B. Birge; op. cit.

[121] As regards printing music from movable types in New England, Metcalf, op. cit., writes, "This book," the *Worcester Collection*, 1786, "was also notable in being the first book in New England printed from music type". In 1767 James Parker had issued from his printing office in Beaver St., N. Y., the psalms of David, edited by Francis Hopkinson, with the music printed above each line. This was the first book printed from music type in America; the melody only was printed, whereas the *Worcester Collection* had all the parts printed on the double staff as is the rule today. Isaiah Thomas who printed the *Worcester Collection* was one of the best-known printers of the time, author of a history of printing, which was reprinted as one of the volumes of the American Antiquarian Society.

CHAPTER SIXTEEN

The Grounds of Music

The collections of psalm-tunes published in New England, from *The Bay Psalm Book* (1698) to those published by William Billings, Daniel Read, Samuel Holyoke and others during the period from 1770 to 1800, contain elaborate instructions in the "Grounds of Music"; even in cases where a few of the more common tunes are bound up with the complete psalms there will be part of a page at least, bearing on the mysteries of 'cliffs' and the 'moods of time'.[122] A musician of our day examining the pages of the "Grounds" would find himself lost in a maze of curious technicalities: *C faut, C solfaut, C solfa;* if *B be flat Mi is in E; minim, crotchet, quaver; the faut cliff; the G solreut cliff; prick'd notes; driving notes; the prick of perfection,* etc. Billings himself objected to that last expression as misleading; for, as he wrote in the preface to the *Singing Master's Assistant* (1778), "a prick of perfection—a dot side of a note—is not well named in my opinion, because a note may be perfect without it; 'point of addition' is the best name."

Any person of musical experience understands very well that a mere study of notational details gives little information as to the actual effect of a performance. In the first place almost everything depends on the tempo or speed, and next on those intangibles that are contributed by musicians to every performance, the *tempo rubato,* the agogic accents, the almost imperceptible but powerfully effective nuances of sound and rhythm impossible even to indicate in the musical notation.[123]

Defects in the style and details of notation in Colonial publications would naturally be expected. Stems of notes were turned the wrong way; their 'flags' were on the wrong side of the stems;

---

[122] See pp. 90-91.
[123] See Appendix N.

the measure might be divided into proportional parts for minims, crotchets, etc., but it was apparently not thought to be necessary for score reading that notes simultaneously sounding should be on the same vertical line. These criticisms are valid as regards collections published even as late as the first decade of the nineteenth century; for example, *The Village Harmony* (1800), *The New England Selection* (1812) and many others. The music pupil of today, weary after fights with his counterpoint teacher over the alto and tenor C clefs, will find them in common use in the psalmbooks and in the collections made for the singing schools; the absolute clearness of the C clef no doubt appealed to the Colonial composer. The counter and alto parts were often written an octave higher than they were to be sounded, although there was occasionally a bothersome uncertainty about this.

It was sometimes definitely stated but more often assumed that the sounds from G on the first line of the staff with the F clef to the G above the staff with the G clef exhausted the material open to composers for vocal music, and these three octaves were referred to as the 'gamut'. The Colonial theorist busied his pupils with involved explanations of the 'gamut', assisted by complicated diagrams showing the principles of solmization, the formation of scales, and the various time or 'meeter' signatures; much was made of 'beating time' and of the 'graces', the 'trill' getting a good deal of attention. There were occasional vagaries of execution, 'transition' being one of the most striking and probably the most devastating of them.

The disposition of the parts in the score and questions as to the actual pitch of the 'counter', at first bother the student of the early collections of tunes. *Urania* (1761) gave the melody to the tenor, one of the later collections to follow the old plan, and it was expected that the women would confine themselves to the treble part, though, as a sex, they justified their reputation for perversity by singing the air. The four measure phrase had not quite the deference paid to it that was later the case; unless the words fell easily into four measures there was seldom any pains taken to secure it.

There was by no means a meticulous care to have musical and verbal accents coincide. Two conspicuous instances of this are the tunes *Windham* (Daniel Read) and *Wells* (Israel Holdroyd, the English composer). Many of the editors of collections tried their hand at these melodies, but always failed to synchronize verbal 'meeter' and musical rhythm; even *Cantica Laudis* (1850), edited by Lowell Mason and G. J. Webb, struggled unsuccessfully with the problem, though it had been solved in 1837 by *The Harmonist,* a Methodist collection.

In the English and American psalmody of the eighteenth century there was much use made of what were called 'graces,' the principal of these, whether one considers the difficulty of execution or the bad effect in performance, being the trill, noted in the music as 'tr.' We find the following discussions of the subject:

(a) In Reverend James Lyon's *Urania,*[124] we are told "the trill or shake is used on all descending prickt crotchets; on the latter of two notes on the same line or space; and generally before a close."

(b) Daniel Bayley[125] quotes from William Tans'ur's *Royal Melody:* "A shake, called the trillo, is (or ought to be) set over any note that is to be shaked or graced; and is the principal grace used in musick; that is, to move your voice distinctly one note, the distance of a whole note; first move slow, then faster by degrees; and by observing this method, you may gain the perfection of it."

(c) William Billings in that lively book, *The Singing Master's Assistant* (1778) writes: "Many ignorant singers take great license from these trills and without confining themselves to any rules they shake all notes promiscuously and they are as apt to tear a note in pieces which should be struck fair and plump as any other. Let such persons be informed that it is impossible to shake a note without going off it, which occasions horrid discords; to remedy which evil they must not shake any note but what is marked with a Trill, and that according to rule, which may be easily learned under a good master."

(d) The *Chorister's Companion,* Simeon Jocelyn (1788), second edition, page 15, defines the shake as "the shaking of two distinct notes upon one syllable as long as the time allows, always beginning with the upper and ending on the lower tone."

(e) Jacob Kimball, Jr., A. B., in *Rural Harmony* (1793), says of the trill, "though a very beautiful grace, is difficult to be acquired

---

[124] *Urania* (1761) perhaps the best known of all psalmodies published in the Middle States.
[125] In his *A New and Complete Introduction to the Grounds and Rules of Music* (1766).

. . . , solos, not full choruses are the proper field for the full display of graces."

(f) In the *American Singing Book*, Daniel Read (1793), page 18, we find, "A trill denotes that the note is to be shaken in an easy and graceful manner. . . . Learners should sing all notes plain until they have arrived to some degree of perfection in the art of music, and even then should be exceedingly careful and not as some do, shake notes to pieces which should be sung plain."

(g) *Bridgewater Collection*, second edition (1804), does not refer to trill or graces in 'grounds', but a few notes are so marked. The editors of collections by this time are fighting shy of the subject, but Henry E. Moore, *New Hampshire Collection* (1835), page viii, disposes of the matter by writing, "What is the use of the trill? It shows that the note should be shaken."

(h) *Songs of Zion*, Thomas Whittemore (1837), page ix, states: "A shake is an ornament or grace, brilliant and elegant. It consists of a quick reiteration, and so forth."

(i) This bird's-eye view of the trill may be concluded by quoting that wise musician, Lowell Mason, page 28, in *Carmina Sacra*, Boston Collection, 1848, who says: "The shake consists of a rapid alternation of two sounds as in the following example. It has no place in common psalmody."

It is a fair inference from these citations that the trill was actually performed where indicated, though possibly by the more adventurous singers and certainly with doubtful success. William Arms Fisher is not of that opinion;[126] he says:

"The sign *tr*, so frequently found, does not indicate a literal trill but an inverted mordent in which the principal note has a single rapid alternation with the auxiliary note above it. Doubtless this ornament was, in part, the basis for the quirks and quavers so characteristic of rural singers a few generations ago."

The 'grace' that must have blurred the harmony, if practiced by any proportion of the singers, is 'transition', thus ingenuously defined:[127]

"Transition is nothing but gracefully gliding from one note to another and renders the melody more agreeable than to pass abruptly from one note to the next."

---

[126] *Old New England Psalm-Tunes*, Oliver Ditson Co., Boston, 1930, p. xiv. 6.
[127] *The American Singing Book*, Daniel Read, 4th ed.

(This word 'abruptly' is too precious.) Using modern terms to describe an obsolete 'grace', 'transition' consists in filling any space between consecutive notes in any voice by adding passing-notes; in the older psalmodies in both England and New England the 'transitions' are often marked as they are to be sung, and are not confined to the air.

Two Italian words, *acciaccatura* and *appoggiatura*, give present day music students trouble, and refer to single 'grace' notes attached to a principal note. To these, the bookish and intellectual Andrew Law gave the name "preparative." He explained them thus:

"these little notes that are sprinkled here and there among the common notes of the tune and add nothing to the time of the bar in which they are sung, but are to be sung in connection with the notes to which they belong. . . . If rightly sung they give to the sounds a turn that is exquisitely nice and delicate. . . . Sometimes they are merely notes of 'transition' from a preceding to a succeeding sound, but more frequently they are considered principal notes, dwelt upon somewhat longer than the notes with which they are connected."

The most troublesome element in the 'grounds' of the New England Collections is that relating to scale formation. Under the name *solmization*, mediaeval theories, particularly as worked out in England, were used in explaining this important matter.[128]

---

[128] See Solmization, Appendix N.

Note. (See p. 83) For a modern use of these disconcerting appellations consult *Acta Musicologica*, vol. xi, 1939, pp. 136-143.

CHAPTER SEVENTEEN

The New England Singing Teacher and His Problems

I have spoken of Andrew Law as of the predominantly intellectual type of musician, who would have done as well in any pursuit where mental acuteness was a requisite. This quality of his is well illustrated in a criticism in the preface to part one of his *The Art of Singing* (1794), second edition which also throws light on the general state of choir singing and suggests a remedy for what he, and I imagine most of us, would regard as the great defect in vocal performance—inferior quality of tone:

> "The tones of our singers are in general, I had almost said universally, rough, hard and dissonant. In a word, our singing in general is very harsh. . . . European compositions aim at variety and energy by guarding against the reiterated use of the perfect cords.[129] . . . great numbers of the American composers on the other hand, as it were on purpose to accommodate their music for harsh singing, have introduced the smooth and perfect cords, till their tunes are all sweet, languid, and lifeless; and yet their tunes, because they will bear better the discord of grating voices are actually preferred in the general run to the great prejudice of much better music produced in this country, and almost to the utter exclusion of genuine European compositions. The singing methods must be improved and the harshness of our singing corrected."

Eight years later than Law, Samuel Holyoke, in the preface to *Columbian Repository* (1802), laid down twenty-eight "necessary rules to be observed in vocal music"; I am quoting these for the reason that they specify quite clearly the faults of chorus singing at the time, and enable us to form a clear idea of how such singing in the Colonial period differed from that of today:

---

[129] By this he must refer to the three principal chords in the major scale which are major chords; and the three in the minor scale, one of which is major.

"1. The first and most necessary rule is to keep the voice steady.
2. Form the voice in as pleasing a tone as possible.
3. Be exactly in tune, for it is not worth while to attempt singing, without a perfect intonation.
4. Practice the swell and diminish frequently.
5. Never force the voice beyond its natural compass or strength. Many singers suppose that they perform well when they exert the full strength of the voice; but this precludes all delicacy of taste and expression, and renders the performance, at best, but a dissonant bawling.
6. Take the part to which your voice is adapted.
7. The acute sounds should never be so forced as to render them similar to shrieks.
8. Avoid all affected gestures and discover no pain or distortion of the mouth or grimace of any kind.
9. Never sing through the nose unless you wish to disgust all who hear you.
10. Attend strictly to the directive terms.
11. Vocalise correctly, that is, give an open and clear sound to the vowels.
12. Words beginning with a vowel ought not to be pronounced as if they began with a consonant. This is a very common error and is occasioned by shutting instead of opening the mouth previously to the pronouncing of vowel sounds.
13. - - - - - - -
14. Such words as *and, of, to, the, a, an, by,* etc. commonly require but little emphasis.
15. Never make a word *plural* when it is written *singular,* nor pronounce it as *singular* when it is written *plural,* by carelessly adding letters when singing which frequently make nonsense.
16. - - - - - - -
17. - - - - - - -
18. - - - - - - -
19. Take breath between the proper passages and in proper time, and never catch the breath in the middle of a word or between syllables.
20. The tones of the voice must be united.
21. - - - - - - -
22. When any part is silent never attempt to sing one, where none was designed; for that will argue that you know better than the composer with respect to the construction of the parts.
23. Accustom yourself to hearing and practicing good harmony which will improve the ear and help to distinguish the elegant from the insipid.

24. Be not solicitous to what you may suppose to be graces till you have learned to judge in some measure of the power of simple notes as applied to any subject.

25. In performing notes connected by a slur the lips should never be closed.

26. Pay attention to the Appogiatures, accidental Sharps, Flats, and Naturals, for if nothing were meant by their introduction they would certainly not have been inserted.

27. Sit upright when you sing, or stand, which is better, that your tones be not injured by any pressure upon the lungs.

28. Let your deportment be decent when you are engaged in performing sacred subjects, an irregular behaviour, especially in worshipping societies, being inexcusable, arguing a mind infallible to solemn impressions, and unfit for engaging in one of the most pleasing parts of the worship of the Supreme Being."

William Billings, a writer of picturesque English, has little patience with people who sing 'off the key':

"Many persons imagine that if they strike within a half note of the true sound, they are tolerably good singers; for they say, 'we strike almost right and therefore we are very excusable'. But let such persons be informed that to strike a note almost well is striking it very ill indeed . . . and those who have not a curious ear I heartily wish could be persuaded to leave the practice of singing to those who have." (*Singing Master's Assistant,* preface.)

All music lovers appreciate the importance of correct timing in a performance, and the New England psalmodies or collection of psalm-tunes made much of time and its 'moods'. In *Elements of Music* (1772) Tans'ur writes:

"It is found by experience that a *Pendulum,* whose Length from the Point of Suspension to the Center of the Ball, is 39 inches and 2 Tenths of an Inch, *Vibrates* or *Beats Seconds,* or 60 Times in one Minute: and for the Certainty and Excellency thereof, it is Called *The Royal Standard. . . . Four* of which *Beats* or Pulses are the Length of a Semibreve, *Two* the Length of a *Minim,* and One the Length of a *Crotchet. . . .* So that *One* Pulse of the *Royal-Pendulum* of a Clock is the Time of 2 *Quavers,* 4 *Semiquavers,* or 8 *Demisemiquavers;* or their respective *Rests.*"

'Common time' had three 'moods', *adagio, largo* and *allegro.* The first was shown by a C; the second, half as fast again as the first, by a C with a stroke through it, and the third as fast again as the *adagio,* by a C inverted and with a stroke, our *alla breve* time. At first it was laid down that a semibreve, or whole note was four seconds, a minim or half note, two seconds long under the C or *adagio* 'mood'; under the C with a stroke, *largo* 'mood' the semibreve would be three seconds long; under the *allegro* 'mood' the semibreve is two seconds long. As the decades move along, directions as to the absolute length of notes become less positive and the music student is reminded that speed is a relative matter. At the risk of boring the reader I must once more quote from the jolly Tans'ur. He is explaining the 'mood' marked 3/2:

> "Suppose the *mood* be marked thus; $^3/_2$, then the 2 underneath imports that the Triple must consist of Minims; and as 2 Minims make a bar in Common-Time, the 3 over the 2 directs that you must sing three minims in triple time to 2 in *Common-Time.* So that each Minim in every bar is one third diminished from those in Common-Time."

This seems to be a peculiar notion, but Tans'ur had a way with him.

The Colonial singing teacher was not above counselling his pupils as to beating time. The preface to the second edition, *Salem Collection,* 1806, gives quaint—and one would think unnecessarily precise—rules for the operation:

> "By beating time is meant a certain regular motion of the right hand or foot. This may and certainly ought to be done without any great flourishing of the arms or stamping with the foot; to avoid which let the singer remember that the design of beating time is neither to offend the eyes or ears of a bystander, but for the direction of himself and others."

The following clear directions for beating were evidently learned in the eighteenth century singing school:

> "For $^4/_4$ time, *one,* let the ends of the fingers fall on some fixed place; *two,* let the wrist fall; *three,* raise the wrist; *four,* lift fingers from the fixed place."

Samuel Holyoke in the preface to *Columbian Repository* (1802) gives five methods of beating time appropriate for the same number of 'moods'. Parsons might well take to heart the following bit, anticipating the transcendental Emerson:

"Whenever I Sing methinks that the very motion I make with my hand to the Musick makes the same Pulse and Impression on my Spirits, it diffuses a Calmness all around me; it delights my Ear and recreates my mind; it fills my soul with pure and heavenly thoughts; so that nothing is near me but peace and Tranquility: And when the Musick sounds sweetest in my ear Truth flows the clearest into my mind."[180]

The pronunciation of the solmization syllables gave rise to some differences in pronunciation. Andrew Law thought that the *i* in *mi* as in *divinity,* should be short, and that *fa, sol* and *la* ought to be sounded *faw, sol* and *law.* Lowell Mason in the 1830 edition of the Boston *Handel & Haydn Society Collection* says, "A in *fa* and *la* may be pronounced as in *Far* or as in *Fall* as the teacher directs." In the *Suffolk Selection* (1807) we are enjoined to say "*me* and not *mi.*" There is always someone about who informs you that he has gone deeper than you into the real merits of a question, and in this case it proves to be Stephen Jencks,[131] who says:

"Let anyone pronounce *fa* or *la,* and they will articulate near the end of the tongue, and the sounds will be flat and insipid. But then pronounce *faw* and *law* and their articulation will have a larger passage through the sounding organs, coming forth like the soft melody of the organ or flute."

This is rather fetching. The book is dedicated to the Teachers of Music and Choristers in the United States. Let us hope that this generosity of dedication was matched by the sale of the book!

SOLMIZATION AS A PROBLEM

Harmony as taught today emphasizes the major and minor scales as entities; the tonic and dominant notes function in definite ways; the first sound in the major scale, *c-d-e-f-g-a-b-c,* has an important use as the root of the tonic chord, that chord (as last chord in a composition) defining the 'key'. It is therefore somewhat difficult to see why *mi,* the seventh sound of the scale should be taken

---

[180] Aaron Williams, the Englishman in *American Harmony* (1771).
[131] See *Laus Deo,* 1818.

as the 'master note'. The system was out of touch with any harmonic background. William Tans'ur[132] has this to say in explanation:

"Why have we in the Scale of Musick, twice *sol,* twice *fa* and twice *la,* and but once *mi?* By Reason *mi* is the Master-Note and guides all the other notes, both above and below it; and when the *mi* is transposed, all other Tones are transposed with it; still lying in their Natural Order according to the Diatonick Scale, etc."

The important point, then, was to find *mi* as the first step in reading music. Thomas Walter states that B is the natural place for it:[133]

"There are other characters in music which serve to vary the place of *mi,* to transpose it from B, its natural place, to some other place or letter. The one is a flat, the other is a sharp. The natural place for *mi* is in B, but if B be flat, *mi* is in E; if B and E be flat, *mi* is in A. If F be sharped *mi* is in F; if F and C be sharped, *mi* is in C."

Tables give the place of *mi* as determined by the sharps or flats key-signature at the beginning of a psalm-tune. It is not clear how the association between the syllables *(mi, fa, sol, la,* etc.) and the notes to which they were related was established; that it was established is proved (a) by the use of the initials of the syllables under the treble and bass of the tunes in *The Bay Psalm Book* and (b) by the use of the same initials in the Reverend John Tufts's book, in this case placed on the lines and spaces of the staff. If the syllables did not assist in realizing the pitch, why use them?

A careful inspection of these initials printed in connection with the trebles and basses of the tunes in *The Bay Psalm Book* (see chapter nine of this book) will show that only in connection with the staff can the syllables show pitch. For example, turn to the tune *Litchfield.* The two first notes are *a* and *d,* sounds of different pitch, yet they are both marked *l (la).* Look at *Windsor,* first phrase: in the treble *f sharp* is called *f (fa)* and in the bass *f natural*

---

[132] "Title page and description: A/New Musical Grammar/and/Dictionary/by William Tans'ur, London, 1756; small 8 vol., pp. xii, 176." See p. 7.
[133] *Introduction to the Grounds and Rules of Music,* Thomas Walter, 12 mo. oblong, Daniel Bayley, Newbury-Port, pp. xxiv-28, 1766, P. 10.

is called f (fa), and that is not all, for b flat in treble and bass becomes f (fa).[134]

We may be pretty sure that there was a great deal of grumbling among music students and practicing musicians at the intricacies of solmization. William Dixon (English musician, 1760-1825) writes in his *Psalmodia Christiana* (ca. 1795):

> "It is usual to learn music by solfaing; but as solfaing is not only very intricate but exceedingly faulty, for 'tis clear that every modulation or alteration of the key the rules for solfaing do not hold, no notice will be taken of the rules in this treatise."

On the other hand, Uriah Davenport (an English musician who published the *Psalm-Singer's Companion* in 1785) thinks:

> "that a voice do the express a Sound best when it pronounceth some Word or Syllable with it; for this Cause, as also for Order and Distinction's sake six syllables were used in former Times, *ut, re, mi, fa, sol, la* and were joined with the seven letters in their scale. But only four of these are necessary Assistants to the right tuning of the Degrees of Sound, the other two *ut* and *re* are superfluous and are therefore laid aside by modern teachers."

So far as the New England composers are concerned the system of solmization, solfaing the major scale as *fa-sol-la-fa-sol-la-mi*, was obsolescent in 1815 or thereabouts and had pretty well disappeared by 1850. As late as 1840 Thomas Hastings, (American musician, 1787-1872), offered a choice of syllables for solfaing—(1) *do-re-mi-faw-sol-law-si-do* or (2) *faw-sol-law-faw-sol-law-mi*. But he seems indifferent to the matter, for he concludes:

> "The Author is aware of some difference of opinion among practical musicians with respect to syllables . . . he cannot . . . attach much

---

[134] This same obliviousness by some Colonial theorists to the difference between a note inflected and uninflected is illustrated by the taking-to-task of William Billings by Ebenezer T. Andrews in the preface to the *Continental Harmony* (1794). Billings was one of the few New England composers who had a clear idea of the circle of keys from C (uninflected) to the keys of seven sharps and seven flats, giving the correct inflected name of *mi*, as G sharp, A sharp, etc. Andrews against Billings runs this way: "If B-E-A-D be flatted *mi* will be G; if F-C-G be sharped G again will be *mi*. Since the seven letters of the alphabet A,B,C,D,E,F,G are all there are in music, there can be seven letter-names for *mi* and therefore only six removes. Billings was wrong in saying there were fifteen keys and fourteen removes." Andrews ignores all the inflections by sharps and flats involved in the seven sharp and seven flat keys, and used properly in naming *mi*.

114

importance to such differences. . . . Although to the vocalist who is unaccompanied by instruments some system of solmization is indispensable."

Lowell Mason in the 1830 edition of the Boston *Handel and Haydn Society Collection* has a lesson on "Solmization in four syllables," *fa-sol-la-mi*. One comes across references to it, indifferent in tone. *The Eastern Lyre* (1842) states that "some use the syllables *fa-sol-la-fa-sol-la-mi*" as if the fact ought to be cited though unimportant, for the sake of record.[135]

MULTIPLICITY OF METHODS OF SCORING A PROBLEM TO THE TEACHER

A piece of music for orchestra or voices at several pitches, as treble, alto, tenor, bass, is said to be 'scored' when the various parts or voices are assembled, each one on its separate five-line staff, the staves arranged above each other. The early psalters *(Genevan, Sternhold & Hopkins, Ainsworth)* printed melodies only. The *Day Psalter* (1563) had the music in parts, each voice having its own book; the same is true of *Este* and *Ravenscroft*, although both printed all four parts on two pages, cantus and tenor (melody) on the left page, altus and bassus on the right. Rimbault and Havergal 'scored' the *Este* and *Ravenscroft* psalters;[136] it is only by 'scoring' that the various parts are brought into a visual relation suitable for study.

The student of psalmody is struck with the great variety of scores that he has to examine. I believe that the following list of the score varieties will be found to include those most used in New England, from Reverend Tufts's *Introduction* to *Urania* (1761), and the 1765 edition of *Tate & Brady*. The *Introduction* used a score of three staves almost entirely, beginning with the top line, cantus (air), medius, bassus. *Urania,* treble (women's voices), counter (written 8ve higher than sung; altos and high tenors), tenor (melody, men's voices), bass. The general understanding of this scoring is that the greatest number of voices is on the tenor, the other parts being less well-supported. *Tate & Brady* (1765)

---

[135] See Appendix I for statements as to the continued use to the present time of the old New England solmization among many of the Southern and Western States.
[136] See their respective reprints.

exhibits nine varieties; these with the number of times used are: cantus, medius, bass (56); cantus, bass (1); counter, tennor, bass (8); altus, discantus, tennor, bass (1); tennor, medius, bass (1); treble, tennor, bass (1); tennor, altus, medius, bass (1); medius, tennor, bass (2); treble, counter tennor, bass (1). This manner of scoring, putting the melody into the tenor, requires a mass of tenor voices, with a full, round bass and a few skilful trebles and counter tenors.

AIR FOR TENOR VOICE

The general situation as regards giving the air to the tenor is well stated by Livingston;[137] he says:

> "the assignment of the melodies to the tenor voice constitutes one of the most distinctive features of the church music of the Reformation period as compared with that of the present day. . . . The ancient practice was based upon the conviction that the larger part of the people would sing the melody only, while the harmony was intended to afford scope for the attainments of the skilful few, and thus became merely a graceful appendage."

It must have become apparent as time went on that the air (the most significant part of the music) was obscured by being thrown into the middle of the tone-mass; a further consideration was that when, as must often have been the case, voices were few, there would be a restriction to melody and bass. Whatever the inducements were by which the singing of the melody was carried over from the tenor to the high women's voices, the effective introduction to the new way was given by John Playford[138] in his *Whole Book of Psalms* (1677). The names of William Damon and Richard Allison might well be associated with this discussion;[139] there is also an interesting instance in *Ravenscroft* that, strange to say, has never been reported.[140]

---

[137] See his reprint of the 1635 *Scottish Metrical Psalter*.

[138] See *Hymns Ancient and Modern*, hist. edn., p. lx, column 1, and foot-notes.

[139] O. Douen (see his *Clément Marot*, Tome Second, p. 367) asserts that Claude Goudimel (c. 1505-1572) has the honor of having anticipated all others in giving the air to the high-pitched voices; this was in Goudimel's *Psautier en harmonie consonante* (1565).

[140] Governor John Endecott (c. 1588-1665) had a copy of *Ravenscroft's Psalmody* (1621); this has come into the possession of the Massachusetts' Historical Society (Boston). The volume is small, upright, not with the original binding (?) but in

Dispossessing the high men's voices from the tenor, that is, from the melody, and giving the melody to the treble voices, as well as writing another part for the tenor, gave rise to a good deal of argument. Echoes of the controversy that this change in scoring and performance must have produced appear in both British and Colonial quarters:

The preface to *British Psalmody* (London, 1825), is of the opinion "that on no account whatever should the air of the four parts when performed together, be sung by other than a treble voice, nor the other parts by other than men's voices." (This would apparently use the male alto instead of the lowest woman's voice.)

The preface to the *Salem Collection* (1805), is very emphatic: "We think we are warranted by the authority of the most eminent composers (certainly by the authority of common sense and analogy in instrumental music) in strongly urging that the air should be sung by treble voices."

John Cole, *Devotional Harmony* (1814), waxes dogmatic: "The propriety of giving the principal air to treble voices is still disputed by some, but those who know anything . . . know that it is right."

Samuel Stanley, in *Twenty-four Tunes* (n.d. but probably about 1800), is clever enough to use the situation for his own purposes: "S.S. particularly requests the Tenor Voices not to sing in the *piano* parts marked in the Air, as they are intended for Treble voices."

An extract from the diary of a musical amateur[141] is apropos: "On . . . I started on a tour to the Western part of Massachusetts. I had many opportunities of observing the customs of musical associations. . . . I found the books used by the choirs were some of the old collections, so noted for spurious melodies and ill-constructed harmonies, and in some instances I found the females still continuing the exploded practice of singing the Tenor (what they improperly called Treble) and that the air was sung by male voices; and in one case I could not but observe a fine, round, full-toned soprano voice, while in

---

excellent condition. The four parts are distributed thus: *Cantus* top of left-hand page; *Tenor, Playn-song* below Cantus; *Medius,* top of r.h.p. page; *Bassus* below the *Medius.* (See *Hymns Ancient and Modern,* hist. ed., p. lvii, for an illustration of this arrangement). All tunes have the *Playn-song* in the Tenor save one, *Canterbury Tune:* in this tune the *Playn-song* is in the *Cantus.* Here is an interesting problem for the musicologist.
[141] *The Euterpiad,* August 3, 1822.

full chorus, attempting to whine out the counter part, with such stentorian lungs as made 'the horrid jargon split the air and drive my nerves asunder'."

The counter was written to be voiced an octave lower; the 'full-toned soprano' must have sung it at pitch, which would have distressed the musical amateur.

It may seem to some of my readers that too much time has been spent in the preceding pages in considering a question of very little practical interest and moreover in the domain of the historian or even the musicologist. This view, I take it, would not only underrate its importance but fail to take into account the influence the clear lines of demarcation of the voices would have on the thinking of the composer, on his technique and on the improvement in the audible effect of music. The three-voiced structure of John Playford could not fail to liberate the musical spirit from the bondage of the confusion of an air sung at its correct pitch by the full voices of men and at the same time, despite protests, an octave higher by the shrill voices of women.

CHAPTER EIGHTEEN

How Were the Psalm-Tunes Sung?

The Reformers gave music back to the people. They translated the psalms into the vernacular, English, French, or German as it happened, selected a simple melody wherever they could find it, and encouraged the people to sing. Indeed the people sang eagerly and their psalms entered into every walk and occupation of life. Prothero's *The Psalms in Human Life*,[142] tells us:

> "When Marot's *Psalms* first appeared, they were sung to popular airs alike by Roman Catholics and Protestants. No one delighted in the *sanctes chansonnettes* more passionately than the Dauphin afterward Henry II; he sang them himself, set them to music, and surrounded himself with musicians who accompanied his voice on the viol or lute. Courtiers adopted their special psalms as they adopted their particular arms, mottoes, or liveries. . . . The Psalms were identified with the everyday life of the Huguenots. Children were taught to learn them by heart; they were sung at every meal in households like that of Coligny; to chant psalms meant in the course of time and in popular language to turn Protestant."

One's curiosity as to the performances of the German religious songs (chorals) at the time of the Protestant Reformation in Germany and the singing in unison of the Genevan reformers in France is natural. What were the standards in tone and execution? Were they anything like the standards of today? Was the singing in four parts? What authentic descriptions of the singing in religious assemblies are accessible? Were the standards in England comparable to those in Germany and Geneva? Was the singing of the psalm-tunes in New England in 1620 as barbarous as we have been told, or at any rate often assumed?

John Calvin had the idea that while psalms were the word of God, hymns were the work of man; consequently the Genevan

---

[142] *Everyman's Library*, pp. 137-8.

melodies were fitted to the metrical version of the psalms. Luther, on the other hand, approved of hymns, and the Reformation in Germany has given us beautiful sacred poems set to the music of the German choral.

We can only imagine just how the singing of the psalms sounded in France, Germany and England, but it seems reasonable, in the absence of contemporary criticism or even description of any sort, to assert that the ordinary worshippers sang with their natural voices, much as congregations do now, except that congregations in France and England sang the melody.

Calvin was opposed to the singing in parts. In unison singing the musical difficulties would be at a minimum; since there would be no complications arising from part-singing, the time would be simple and probably Calvin's insistence on the purity, religiously speaking, of the words would operate to concentrate attention on them and the rhythm would easily and freely follow their meter. This is of course mere conjecture, but one has only to sing through one of the Genevan psalms to appreciate the fascination or even overwhelming effect of a large body of people singing in unison. We must remember that these psalm melodies, many of them mediaeval in origin, were quite complete in themselves, not needing the color or sonority coming from harmony.

It may with some truth be said that in congregational singing we must consider two forces in operation—the wishes of the great majority of voices that make up the congregation, musically speaking, and the urge of the really musical, who number those who have high-pitched voices and those who have low-pitched voices.

Ordinary music-lovers will need the melody pitched in medium range and will wish to sing the melody. Calvin was right in sensing that the strength of the music lay in the melody.[143]

A smaller section of a congregation, but the musically intelligent part, will want to sing in parts, which means that the treble

<hr />

[143] The second volume of O. Douen's *Clément Marot et le Psautier Huguenot* contains 235 pages of harmonized versions of the various psalm melodies by C. Jannequin (1547), L. Bourgeois (1547), J. Louis (1555), Philibert Jambe-de-Fer (1559), Claude Goudimel (1565), Roland de Lattre (1594), known also as Orlando di Lasso, Claudin le Jeune (1564), and nine other composers of the period, in from three to eight parts. Evidently there must have been singing in parts somewhere and sometime, notwithstanding Calvin's dislike of anything beyond melody singing in worship.

part must be pitched high, too high for the ordinary voices to be comfortable. As music in the twentieth century goes, however, we favor singing in parts for the hymns. Lowell Mason, a wise man in his generation, demanded music in unison, with the harmonies sung by the choir; and his idea will now and again find utterance. (See preface of *National Psalmist*, 1848.)

We have one bit of contemporary testimony to the actuality of part-singing, from the *Scottish Psalter* of 1635:

"John Durie cometh to Leith at night the third September, 1582. Upon Tuesday, the fourth of September, as he is coming to Edinburgh there met him at the Gallowgreen 200, but ere he came to the Netherbow their number increased to 400; but they were no sooner entered but they increased to 600 or 700, and within short space the whole street was replenished even to Saint Geiles kirk; the whole number was esteemed to 2,000. At the Netherbow they took up the 124 Psalme, 'Now Israel may say' and sung in such a pleasant tune in four parts known to the most part of the people, that coming up the street all bareheaded until they entered the Kirk, with such a great sound and majestie, that it moved both themselves and all the huge multitude of the beholders . . . with admiration and astonishment."

It may be ventured, however, that in the case of the Durie march probably all the people knew the melody, which was the part sung by the majority of the people, even if there were enough high and low voices among the remainder to make up the four parts. This is one of the most remarkable incidents of psalm-singing by a large number of people, properly authenticated, that we have. The "Old 124th" is found in modern hymnals under the name "Toulon," but the five phrases of the original by Bourgeois are shortened by the omission of one.

It seems legitimate to think that these harmonizations of the melodies by Goudimel and others pretty accurately mirrored the vocal capabilities of the reformers. The settings are largely note against note, with little or no chromaticism, flavored now and again with modal harmony, but simple rhythmically. There would seem to be no reason why those who essayed a performance of these arrangements could not make a good showing. With a choir of several hundred singers these old tunes in four parts would give a great effect.

While the *Calvin Psalter* had a great variety of meter the *Sternhold & Hopkins* (1562) used very largely what was known as the ballad meter, that is a stanza of eight lines, 8.6.8.6.8.6.8.6. (D.C.M.) or of four lines, 8.6.8.6. (C.M.). This had a certain effect on the performance of the English psalter; Common Meter stanzas were short, the tunes had greater symmetry than the Genevan tunes with lines of 11 and 12 syllables, and were therefore more easily learned and longer remembered. The Double Common Meter tunes did not have so great an advantage over the Genevan tunes as regards ease of acquisition, but they were symmetrical and often of great interest. These English tunes suggest a good degree of choral technique; we ought not to forget in this connection, that the Elizabethan period was in full swing when the Virgin Queen called back the exiled Reformers to their native land.

John Strype (1643-1737) in *Annals of the Reformation* comments on the singing of the psalms but he does not give any particulars of performance or standards of performance that would enlighten us.

> "After sermon they all sing in common a psalm in metre as it seems was frequently done, the custom having been brought in from abroad by the exiles."

This was a custom about 1599.

In 1644, this being twenty-three years after the publication of Ravenscroft's book, Thomas Mace, writes graphically about the Royalist psalm-singing during the eleven weeks' siege of York, England (1644):

> "Now here you must take notice that they had then a custom in that church (which I heard not of in any other cathedral) which was that always before the sermon, the whole congregation sang a psalm together with the quire and organ, and you must know that there was then a most excellent-large-plump-lusty-full-speaking organ. . . . This organ, I say, when the psalm was set before the sermon, being let out into all its fulness of stops together with the vast concording unity of the whole congregation. . . . I was so transported . . . . that there was no room left in my whole man, viz. body soul and spirit, for anything below divine and heavenly raptures."[144]

---

[144] For the full quotation see Scholes, *The Puritans and Music*, op. cit., pp. 272, 273.

There is general agreement among writers that psalm singing was not only a common but a popular pastime in private houses during Elizabeth's reign, and for some twenty years after. It may be taken for granted, however, that there was little if any harmonized singing of psalm-tunes in the ordinary churches in the times of Elizabeth and the Stuarts, and unison singing led by the parish clerk was recognized as the most suitable way of rendering the praises of God in the sanctuary. (Lightwood, *Hymn-tunes and Their Story.*) Was this a prejudice against singing in parts as a mere amusement? Or was it thought the meaning of the words would come out better if melody only were sung? If it was a prejudice, was it inherited from Geneva?

Queen Elizabeth was musical, and in the splendid outburst of energy that marked her reign, poetry and song flourished greatly. The Queen herself maintained a fine choir for her Chapel Royal, and at many cathedrals the tradition of anthems and musical services was carried on.[145]

Reverend W. T. Whitley, M.A., LL.D., gives an entertaining account of the Elizabethan psalm-singing at Kenilworth, away from cathedrals:[146] "The forenoon occupied as for the Sabbath day in quiet and vacation from work, and in divine service and preaching at the parish church. The afternoon in excellent sweet music of sundry sweet instruments, and in dancing of lords and ladies. . . . Sometimes I foot it with dancing, now with my gittern, and also with cittern, then at the virginals."[147]

The custom of 'lining-out', which was established in England and spread to Scotland and America, was hurtful to hymn-singing; it broke the continuity of the thought and the music by making a stop after every line (phrase) while the clerk or precentor read the next line. Doctor Millar Patrick[148] says that:

"Singing of the psalms, inexpressibly dreary, was made worse by the importation from England of the practice of 'lining'—the precentor reading or intoning each line before it was sung. Such a practice, necessary where the people had few or no psalters or where they were in general illiterate, was absurd in Scotland, where the people could

---

[145] John S. Bumpus, *English Cathedral Music*, p. 4.
[146] *Congregational Hymn-singing in England*, J. M. Dent & Sons, Ltd., London, 1933.
[147] *England under the Tudors*, pp. 78, 81.
[148] *Manual of Church Praise*, Church of Scotland, Edinburgh, 1932, p. 43.

read; yet it established itself so firmly in favor that in some cases congregations suffered serious secessions when it began to be abandoned."

Lightwood[149] gives this description of an obsolete practice:

"The 1645 Westminster Assembly, as it is called, ordained that 'where many of the congregation cannot read, it is convenient that the minister, or some other fit person appointed by him and the other officers, do read the psalm, line by line before the singing thereof'. . . . Our Puritan forbears were not overblessed with a sense of the ludicrous, or they would have been much exercised to sing, say, verse 3 of the 50th Psalm with decorum. For this is what would take place. The Clerk would give out the first line, 'The Lord will come and He will not'— and then the congregation would repeat the extraordinary statement. Then the clerk would read, 'Keep silence, but speak out'—and this paradoxical remark would then be solemnly sung by the congregation. . . . This custom continued in use for many years. The Scotch did not take to it kindly at first, for they could not see why they should be made to suffer merely because their English brethren could not read; but by degrees it became almost a second nature with them, and in the end they were loath to give up the custom . . . it gradually gave way to two lines being read at once, which remained the practice for some years after 1860, especially among Nonconformists, who, at any rate in country districts, retained the custom of giving out two lines at a time until quite recently."

In 1779 a committee of the First Congregational Church, Sturbridge, Massachusetts, made a report to the church concerning 'singing by rule', 'Reading line by line', etc.:

"Another matter of discouragement is the Singers not having Liberty to Sing once a Day without reading line by line &c as to this, the Singers as Individuals have a Right to Private Judgment. they togather think that is best. the Church has the same Right. wee must strive to Enlighten each other, & hope we shall be lead to do right. Nothing is more common than opposition and Discouragement in a good work."

That the good people in Sturbridge were not invariably considerate in their treatment of the singers is shown by a second paragraph:

"Another thing mentioned by the Singers is their Persons & Characters being injuriously Treated; as to this wee know not the Persons nor

[149] Op. cit., p. 80.

the Particular Circumstances that have attended their offenses: wee hope those Persons will Seriously reflect on their Conduct. . . ."

On their side the singers were not blameless. The report goes on:

"With respect to the matters of uneasiness in the minds of some Relative to the proceedings of the Singers in some respects Since the late Endeavours of Learning to Sing by Rule in our Congregation in the first place the Singers Ariseing to Set the Psalm or Strike the Tune when the Quethiser or Quethisers, who were orderly Introduced to do that Duty being Present attempting to do their Duty were Interrupted, & this of the Singers was not as wee Suppose don on a Sudden by Surprise, but by before Determination: further their proceeding to Sing without reading by line, no previous notice being given to thos whose Duty it was to read, & haveing no vote of the Church passed to Sing without Reading."

It does not take a vivid imagination to reconstruct that scandalously amusing scene in the House of the Lord.[150]

There is a difference of opinion as to the speed of singing the psalms. Dr. Millar Patrick (op. cit., p. 44) thinks that every circumstance helped to establish a slow, drawling kind of singing. On the other hand, Livingston[151] inclines to the belief that the singing of the psalms was brisk. In some cases it was directed that long psalms should be 'sung whole', which is inconsistent with slow speed. "The assemblage that escorted Durie," continues Livingston, "would naturally have fallen into a march step" and that is inconsistent with slow speed. It may also be presumed that Reformers, having been trained to the prose chanting of the Romish Church, could not at once sink into a slow and insipid rate of movement. In the preface to Havergal's *Old Church Psalmody* (1849) we find:

"Singers formerly sang with good speed. A dozen verses reduced to six by a double tune formed a very moderate portion for one occasion. Speed was necessary. Dr. Gauntlett (1805-1876), who edited *Dr. Watts's Own Tune Book* (J. Hart, London, n.d.) states that Dr. Watts preferred the psalmody of the antient churches, and disliked the heavy motion, tedious syllables, the tiresome extent and the no-mean-

---

[150] The entire report is quoted in George H. Haynes's sketch of the church, The Davis Press, Worcester, 1910.
[151] Op. cit., p. 51.

ing style of singing. He desired a greater speed in the motion of the voice as more intelligible to others, more delightful to ourselves and more after the manner of antient usage."

On the other hand Sir Richard Terry states:

"It is a fact that the tunes (of the *Scottish Psalter*) should be sung slowly."[152]

Musicians are always sceptical as to the merits of congregational singing anywhere and at any time. Mace's enthusiasm at the singing in York Minster is an exception. The learned Doctor Burney, the friend of Samuel Johnson, in his *History of Music* (1789), wrote a severe criticism of such singing, calling it 'bawling out'.

"The greatest blessing to lovers of music in a parish church is to have an organ in it sufficiently powerful to render the voices of the clerk & those who join in his outcry wholle inaudible. Indeed all reverence for the psalms seems to be lost by the wretched manner in which they are sung."

This be it noted is contemporary criticism and can not be ignored.

Psalm-singing in New England in the seventeenth century is not described with any precision in records of the day, although we find here and there something. The whole situation would serve to show that the Colonists took with them the singing styles and habits of their contemporaries in England; faults and virtues, in the nature of the cases, must have been alike.

Curwen *(Studies in Worship Music,* first series) has an interesting chapter on New England Psalmody, pp. 58-59, quoting from the Reverend T. Symmes of Bradford, Massachusetts:

"There are many persons of credit now living, children and grand-children of the first settlers of New England, who can very well remember that their ancestors sang by note, and that they learned to sing of them and that they have more than their bare words to prove that they speak the truth; for any of them can sing tunes exactly by note which they learned of their fathers and they say that they sang all of the tunes in the same manner. . . ."

Symmes was writing in 1720. It was unfortunately the fact that through the use of grace notes, the trill, 'transition' and other im-

---

[152] See the *Scottish Psalter* of 1635, R. R. Terry, p. XII.

provised ornaments of the melody, the tune itself became disguised; he pleads for a return of the plain notes of the originals as set down in the psalm-book; and for the establishment of singing schools.

Congregational singing, as described by Reverend Thomas Walter in 1721, was indeed very bad. He speaks of eight or ten psalm-tunes as being the maximum number in use, while some churches use little more than half that number. He has heard *Oxford* tune sung in three churches with as much difference as there could possibly be between as many different tunes . . . "the psalm-singing sounding like five hundred different tunes roared out at the same time, and so little in time that they were one or two words apart; so hideous as to be bad beyond expression." (See Curwen, op. cit., and Daniel Bayley's edition of Walter's *Grounds and Rules,* 1766.) If the singing in church was as bad as all that it is strange that such an offense against public decency had not been condemned and attended to before. It would have been, had communal action, inspired by a desire for improvement on the part of the worshippers in a mass, been taken. We are likely to forget that in other matters of public etiquette the times were crude.

Cotton Mather (1663-1728), contemporary of Tufts and Walter, has this to say:

> "It has been found in some of our congregations that in length of time their singing has degenerated into an odd noise that has had none of what we want a name for than any regular singing in it; whereby the Celestial Exercise is dishonored and indeed the Third Commandment is trespassed upon."[153]

Mather's criticism by reason of its moderation and gentle sarcasm is more effective than Walter's violence.

Were Instruments Used with the Voices?

It is generally understood that both in England and America instruments were used in conjunction with the psalm-singing in church worship; but definite information is hard to find. In the New England collections of psalm-tunes for churches or singing-

---

[153] *History of King's Chapel in Boston,* F. W. R. Greenwood, Boston, 1833.

schools there are no parts for instruments nor definite statements as to their employment; here and there one will note the words 'organ', 'symphony', 'sym.', these implying an instrumental interlude or prelude.

Such indications are found more often in anthems than in psalm-tunes. Thus in the *Columbian and European Harmony* or *Bridgewater Collection of Sacred Music* (by Bartholomew Brown A.M. and others, second edition, February, 1804), there are a few indications of the use of instruments for accompaniment:

> *Pentecost* has an eight-bar duet for Treble—Tenor, Treble—Counter accompanied by Bass and Bassoon.
> *Hanover* has sixteen bars of Bass accompaniment.
> *Litchfield* at one place has "organ soft", which seems to imply that the organ had a part.
> *Cheshunt* by Doctor Arnold has a four-bar 'Sym' (Symphony) for four instruments, probably two violins, bass and bassoon; one 'Sym' of eight bars; a bass accompaniment of twenty-eight bars; and three more 'Sym's' of four bars each, all Symphonies for four instruments at least.
> *Upton* (Doctor Arnold) has a line marked 'Organ' which apparently runs straight through 64 bars as an obbligato; there are three 'Sym's' of two bars each, for three instruments, violins and bass.
> *Abingdon* (Doctor Arnold) has an instrumental interlude of six measures for two violins and bass.
> *Amesbury* (Doctor Arnold) has throughout its five pages a bass obbligato to a treble and alto duet; also three 'Sym's' (Symphony) of two bars each. These pieces quoted are of some length and give a presumption of what would be found in other collections.

The indications of instrumental accompaniments are naturally rare in the ordinary psalm-tune.

> In *New York Selection* (1816, page 99) an interlude of three bars is described as 'symphony'.
> As late as 1828 the North Congregational Society of Newburyport, Massachusetts, still used a violin and 'bass-viol' with other stringed instruments to accompany the hymns.[154]
> *The Hartford Collection* (1807, page 127), tune *Mansfield*, has two bass staves, one labelled "instrumental bass."
> The *Newburyport Collection* (Exeter, 1807) has several indications of the use of instruments in accompaniments; such notations are occasionally met with elsewhere.

---

[154] Joshua Coffin's *History of Newburyport*, Vol. I, p. 280.

In 1842, the First Congregational Church at Sturbridge, Massachusetts, had seats in the gallery for the singers and instrumentalists; of the latter there were violins, a flute, a clarinet, a bass viol and a double bass.

It is usually supposed that the bass viol was the old viol da gamba, a six-stringed instrument of the viol family. On the other hand Tans'ur states that the bass viol is the violoncello. The double bass, used in the modern orchestras, is a viol, for it has sloping shoulders, a flat back, and of unequal thickness from back to belly. It is not, however, the 'bass viol'. Dunstan[155] gives bass viol as the common term for violoncello.

It is probable that an intensive search through all the New England collections in libraries like the Lowell Mason Library, Yale University, and that of the Massachusetts Historical Society might collect sufficient data to widen our knowledge; a search through church records would also help even more.

It may occur to some readers that the New Englanders had too few instruments, strings and wood-wind, to be able to offer assistance in the psalmody. So far as I am aware it is not possible to fix any date at which instrumental assistance in church music was an accomplished fact. The Puritans, at any rate, had a wider acquaintance with household instruments of music than is generally supposed. The *Boston News-Letter* for April 16-23, 1716, had this advertisement:

"To be sold at Dancing School of Mr. Enstone in Sudbury Street, near the Orange Tree, Boston, a choice Collection of Musical Instruments, consisting of Flageolets, Flutes, Haut Boys, Bass Viols, Bows, Strings, Reeds for Haut Boys, Books of Instruction for all these Instruments, Books of Ruled Paper. NOTE. Any Person may have all those Instruments of music mended or Virginalls and Spinetts Strung and tuned at a reasonable rate, and likewise may be taught by a true and easier method than has been before."

This advertisement seems to imply a considerable number of people, pupils and professional musicians to be catered for. Sonneck[156] is of the opinion that the Boston concert season began in 1751; and this, too, implies a communal maturity in music that might

---

[155] *A Cyclopedic Dictionary of Music*, Ralph Dunstan, Mus. Doc., J. Curwen and Sons, Ltd., 1925.

[156] Op. cit., p. 251.

find pleasure and satisfaction in playing in church, even in the humble task of accompanying the choir and congregation in the singing.

In imagining the players functioning as psalmody assistants we can only conjecture the ways in which they might help. The bass-viol might give the pitch either alone or with the violin. The various instruments would double in those parts that were naturally related to their compass: the bass viols would double the vocal bass, perhaps an octave lower when practicable; the violin would double the treble part or the bass viol the tenor part during the period when the tenor had the tune. This would take care of all the tunes in *The Bay Psalm Book,* which were all 'scored' for air and bass. John Playford's *Whole Book of Psalms* (1677), would have a Medius part, and this might be played by a second violin. Of course this is all pure invention on my part, but its plausibility will be admitted.

The organ has been the occasion or at any rate the center of much acrimonious discussion in regard to the moral right, appropriateness or usefulness of instrumental help in psalmody. Much of this debate has been associated with Scotland. Doctor Millar Patrick[157] tells us that "in pre-Reformation Scotland organs were in use, though only in a few special churches. . . . At the Reformation antipathy to them was aroused, and what happened is illustrated by what took place in Aberdeen, where the Kirk Session in 1574 directed that the organ should with all expedition 'be removit out of the kirk and made profeit of to the use and support of the puir'."

"King James in 1617 had one built in the Chapel Royal in Holyrood but . . . the instrument was maisterfullie broken down . . . bot the haill chaplains, choristers and musicianes dischargit, and the costly organes altogedder destroyit and unusefull. . . ."

It was current among the people that "the Organes came first, now the Images, and ere long they should have the Masse". It was a long fight and came to its conclusion in Scotland as late as 1883, the General Assembly of the Free Church finding "that there is nothing in the Word of God or the Constitutions and laws of

[157] Op. cit.

the Church, to preclude the use of instrumental music in church."
Doctor Percy A. Scholes[158] quotes Calvin:

"It would be a too ridiculous and inept imitation of papistry to decorate the churches and to believe oneself to be offering God a more noble service in using organs and the many other amusements of the kind. . . . All that is needed is a simple and pure singing of the divine praises coming from the heart and mouth and in the vulgar tongue . . . instrumental music was tolerated in the time of the Law because the people then were in infancy."

Doctor Scholes sums up the whole matter thus:

"With the whole Eastern Church barring the church organ, the Church of Rome officially reflecting on its abuse, Luther only lukewarm to it, Calvin objecting to it and many good Anglican dignitaries doing the same, it will be seen that at this period the instrument was under a cloud."

In the eighteenth century the organ had gained in favor as a church instrument, John Wesley describes in his journal a Lutheran service he attended in Amsterdam. There was a long voluntary on the organ, closed with a hymn sung by all the people sitting; a second hymn to the organ, all the people sitting; a third hymn; the creed in rhyme; another hymn. Wesley was much surprised at the organ.[159] Wesley, later, had an experience with the organ in church that gave him a great respect for its devotional use:

"We administered the Sacrament to about thirteen hundred persons. While we were administering, I heard a low, soft, solemn sound, just like that of an Aeolian harp. It continued five or six minutes and so affected many that they could not refrain from tears. It then gradually died away."[160]

It was in the same century that in the Church of St. Magnus, just on the south side of London Bridge, an organ was installed (1712) having some of its pipes enclosed in a box with movable shutters or louvres; this is now a part of a large organ called "the swell."

[158] Op. cit., pp. 336 et seq.
[159] Dr. W. T. Whitley, op. cit., p. 135.
[160] Scholes, op. cit., p. 348.

With the exception of the organ built for the Boston Music Hall by Walcker in 1863, the organ given by Thomas Brattle, Esq. to the Brattle Square Church in Boston in the eighteenth century has attracted the greatest interest. Mr. Brattle gave the Brattle Square Church the first chance at the organ, but on July 24, 1714, they refused it, and it was accepted by the King's Chapel, on August 3, the same year. It was voted by the gentlemen of King's Chapel:

"that the 'Orgins' be accepted by the Church as given by Thomas Brattle, Esq., and that Mr. Myles answer Mr. William Brattle's letter concerning the same."[161]

A few days afterward the organ was brought into the church but not erected for several months. In 1756 a new organ was brought from London at an expense of six hundred and thirty-seven pounds sterling, the Brattle organ being sold to St. Paul's, Newburyport, where it remained for eighty years, finding then a permanent resting place in St. John's Church, Portsmouth, New Hampshire.

The *Oxford Companion to Music*[162] (page 664) has this to say about early organs in America:

"The first organ in America may have been that in Gloria Dei Church (Swedish) (1694) in Philadelphia. In 1700 the Episcopal Church at Port Royal, Virginia, had an organ."

Henry C. Lahee, the author of a series of popular historical handbooks—covering singers (1898); violinists (1899); pianists (1900); opera in America (1901); organists (1902); opera-singers (1912)—in a letter to *The Christian Science Monitor* (December 13, 1938) states:

". . . In the research work that I did for *The Annals of Music in America,* I found that a pipe organ was imported in 1700 and placed in the Episcopal Church in Port Royal, Virginia; this was undoubtedly the first organ used in public worship, for the Brattle organ was not so used until 1713. . . . The Port Royal organ after many vicissitudes found a home in the Smithsonian Institute, Washington, D. C., where it can be seen. . . ."

---

[161] Greenwood, op. cit., p. 74.
[162] See *Grove, Dictionary of Music, American Supplement,* article "Organ."

The next thing after installing such an important instrument as an organ is to find someone to play it. According to J. W. D. Greenwood:

> "Mr. Enstone, a person of sober life and conversation entered on his duties as organist of King's Chapel about Christmas, 1714 . . . the music of the Chapel must now have been a great and attractive, though a very offensive novelty; for there is no doubt that this organ was the first ever heard in public worship in all New England."

We do not hear whether Mr. Enstone continued to be a person of "sober life and conversation", but we do know that in ten years, in 1724, it was:

> "Voted that Mr. Nathaniel Gifford be organist for the ensuing year, and that he play a Voluntary before the first lesson and attend the Church upon all Holy Days."[163]

As a musical instrument capable of adding color and intensification to the worship music of the early eighteenth century we can not say very much of the organ; it had, of course, its power of sustaining the tone, at any rate so long as the humble 'organ pumper' attended to his job; but its dynamic range was small and its emotional range compared with the instrument of today, limited.

The pipes were put under expression not much before 1712, the pedals, although invented about 1325, were not available, in England at any rate, much before the middle of the eighteenth century. Handel's concertos show little indication of a functioning pedal, although his great contemporary J. S. Bach (1685-1750) wrote for an organ embodying much that makes the instrument indispensable for church today. The Choral Preludes of Bach are now accessible to all organists; but Preludes, no doubt written and played for the psalm-tunes sung in English churches in the eighteenth century, are seldom found.

See Starling Goodwin's *Complete Organist's Pocket Companion* (about 1725?), Lowell Mason Library (at the Library of the School of Music), Yale University, which illustrates more or less clearly what the English player did to play over the psalm-tune.

[163] Op. cit., p. 128.

Goodwin's preludes are very florid by reason of trills, turns, and scales in profusion, but the interludes are very neat.

Doctor Percy A. Scholes, in speaking about the Reverend K. H. MacDermott's *Sussex Church Music in the Past* (Chichester, 1923), calls attention to the fact that "everything else in Sussex church life from architecture to old brasses, from episcopal visitations to 'church ales', is to be found lengthily treated in books, but music is almost absent." That has some bearing on the general indifference to or knowledge about music in New England in Colonial days.

Sonneck quotes from the constitution of the Essex Musical Association the regulation that there was to be an annual "musical exhibition" at which the performances were to be vocal and instrumental with bass viols, flutes and violins as "Instruments used at present."[164] This was from 1797 on. Samuel Holyoke was the founder of this Association, and the *Massachusetts Compiler* was their standard collection. It is not unreasonable to infer that the instruments named were taken along to church Sundays to use with the singing.

Although unison singing of the psalms would be helped by the instruments capable of playing the air either in unison or octave higher (Violin or Flute) or an octave lower (Bass-Viol), organized instrumental support would be necessary in the case of singing in two parts (treble and bass, as in *The Bay Psalm Book*, 1696) or three parts (cantus, medium, and bassus) as in Tufts's *Introduction*, or even earlier in J. Playford's work (1677). That is to say, the rise of instrumental accompaniment for the psalms synchronized with the rise of part-singing.

---

[164] Op. cit., p. 321.

CHAPTER NINETEEN

Hymns, Hymn-Tunes and Hymn-Singing

Do you know what a hymn is? It is singing with the praise of God. If you praise God and do not sing, you utter no hymn. If you sing and praise not God, you utter no hymn. If you sing anything which does not pertain to the praise·of God, tho in singing you praise, you utter no hymn. —*St. Augustine.*

This precise definition of a hymn sufficed for the church until changes took place giving a broader meaning; the store of sacred lyrics that has resulted from the expansion of church life has passed pretty generally into use in public worship. The early psalmodies of *Sternhold & Hopkins* (1562, in its complete form), and *Este* (1592) contained, besides the complete psalms in meter, versions of the *Veni Creator, The Humble Sute Of A Sinner, Venite Exultemus, Te Deum, Magnificat, Nunc Dimittis,* and others; but these are not sacred lyrics in the same sense in which are the many noble verses of Watts, C. Wesley, or Faber. In fact, *Sternhold & Hopkins,* lasting practically for one hundred and fifty years, became archaic and failed completely to serve its public. *Tate & Brady* (1696) soon superseded the *Sternhold & Hopkins* version and became the 'new version', the two versions stepping along side by side for a few years or until *Tate & Brady* had the field entirely to itself. No wonder that singing languished in the Church of England services. Familiarity had bred dislike and even contempt for the old psalmody in its uncouth or positively vulgar phraseology.

It is not surprising to find that when John Wesley entered on his evangelistic work in 1735 one of the first things to which he turned his attention was the singing; it must be remembered that at this time the people, clergymen and laymen, later called Methodists, were communicants of the Church of England. The apathy of the Church in regard to congregational song was remarkable. Public interest was small. All the musical strength was concentrated at the cathedrals and other places where a choir of professional musicians was maintained. Anthems were written, canticles were set, chants were composed for the prose psalms, but rarely were new tunes composed for the metrical psalms.[165] In a general way as regards hymn-singing we may say that the Non-conformists in England showed quite as much interest as the Anglicans. Here is the place to mention Isaac Watts (1674-1748) and Charles Wesley (1707-1788) as prolific authors of hymns and sacred lyrics and therefore in large measure responsible for the growth of this movement.[166]

Before Doctor Watts published his psalms and hymns the Congregationalists first used the Scottish version of the Psalms, and afterwards the versions by Doctor Patrick of Charterhouse. The tunes commonly sung were certain favorites out of the old Psalter tunes which up to the death of Charles I had always been printed with the old version of Psalms. (That is, the *Sternhold & Hopkins,* 1562.) Of these the German tunes were never popular, the Anglicans were the great favorites, together with some of the Scottish and one or two of the Lutherans. The three most popular were *Old Windsor,* which was the Catholic Christmas hymn or tune, *Old Hundred,* the Huguenot melody, and *Old Martyrs,* a genuine Scottish tune. Doctor H. J. Gauntlett in the preface to *Doctor Watts' Own Tune Book* states: "There were no three-two tunes such as were plentiful in the seventeenth century. Some few came up in Watts's time and one of his is in his book. The common time tunes were the favorites and indeed all the tunes howsoever written were sung in equal time, a syllable to a note." This statement needs proof.

"Of all the old Psalter tunes Doctor Watts enumerates the tunes of C.M., L.M., and S.M., also Old 50th, 112th, 113th, 117th, 148th and the new tune to his version of the 50th Psalm. From these Francis Hoffman engraved the melodies fitted to the metres most

---

[165] Whitley, op. cit., p. 112.
[166] Whitley, op. cit., chapter vii. Also *Hymns Ancient and Modern,* hist. edn., chap. xv.

generally in use. Doctor Watts preferred the Psalmody of the antient churches, and disliked the heavy motion, tedious syllables, the tiresome extent and the no-meaning style of singing. He desired a greater speed in the motion of the voice as more intelligible to others, more delightful to ourselves and more after the manner of antient usage."[167]

C. Wesley wrote about 6500 hymns. Watts also had a great popularity in both England and America, for the impetus given in the Old Country passed quickly to the New. Recalling the free use of hymns by Luther in Germany in the fifteenth and sixteenth centuries it seems strange, considering the general use today in English and American hymnals of the choral melodies and translations of German hymnology, that hymn-singing should be as late as about 1740 in getting its first vogue in England and America.[168]

J. Spencer Curwen notes: "We must call to mind that hymns, heartily sung by a whole congregation, were an unknown element in public worship at the time when Wesley and Whitefield's work began. We are so accustomed to regard congregational singing as an essential of public devotion that it requires an effort to realize this fact. . . . Dissenters were slow to receive hymns, even those of Watts's, and Church people did not know them at all. John Wesley, although like his brother Charles, a member of the Church of England, in describing the ordinary service of the parish Church refers to 'the drawl of the parish clerk', the 'screaming of the charity children', and 'scandalous doggerel of Hopkins and Sternhold.' It is easy to understand how welcome the new hymn-tunes were, with their pulsating, secular rhythms, their emotional repetitions, the fugal tunes, the iterations of words in cumulative sequences after the 'sleep' of formalism. . . . The Methodists with their hymns and their singing burst like heralds of new life. Crowds were drawn to their services simply by the irresistible charm of the music. To sing hymns was to be a Methodist. The Independents were not long in joining the movement, the Church of England pursuing its conservative way."[169]

It was to improve the singing in 1742 that John Wesley pub-

[167] Dr. Watts' Own Tune-Book, ed. by Dr. H. D. Gauntlett, J. Hart, London, n.d. A copy is in the Lowell Mason Library, Yale University.
[168] J. T. Lightwood, op. cit., p. 121.
[169] Studies in Worship-Music, first set, op. cit., p. 24, et seq.

137

lished the *Foundery Tune-Book*, named in allusion to the King's Foundery, Windmill Street, London, not far from where Wesley's Chapel now stands. The Duke of Marlborough's cannon needed at Blenheim were cast at this foundry. One day in 1716 an explosion wrecked the building and it was abandoned. For years it lay derelict, getting more ruined and rat-ridden every year. John Wesley about this time was looking for a permanent home for his work and himself; he bought the place for one hundred-fifteen pounds, expending another eight hundred in making it habitable. This was in 1739. Thus came the first Methodist meeting-house in London.

Lightwood (op. cit.) describes the *Foundery Tune-Book* as "one of the worst printed books ever issued from the press; and not only is the printing bad, but the work is full of the most extraordinary mistakes, such as wrong bars and notes and impossible musical phrases. . . . Of course, all these mistakes ruined the sale of the book, and no second edition was ever printed." In 1882 the *Foundery Tune-Book* was given a photo-electrotype reprint of 36 pages; the music takes a space of three and one quarter inches by five, the original plates being, of course, somewhat larger. The music is type-set, melodies only, and is a hodge-podge of the good and the simply outlandish; one could imagine no greater contrast than afforded by a comparison with the melodies of the 1563 edition of the *Sternhold & Hopkins* psalter or those of the 1612 *Ainsworth* psalter. Yet both musically, as a key-book, and historically, as showing the violence and character of the break with the old psalmody, the collection is of great value.[170]

Owing to the close connection between Great Britain and America we have not felt the need of making our own sacred lyrics for church use; we have had no poets of the facile invention and spiritual power of Watts and C. Wesley turning their genius to devotional ends. However, we may claim for our nineteenth cen-

---

[170] The Hartford Seminary Foundation Library, Hartford, Conn., has a copy of the reprint. Bound up with it is a copy of the 1737 Collection/of/Psalms/and hymns/Charlestown/printed by James Timothy; pp. vi-77. An analysis of key and time is to be noted. There are 43 tunes, 42 with names, *First German Tune, Bedford Tune, Savannah Tune, Jericho Tune*. Of the 42 tunes, 27 are in major keys and 15 in minor. 23 tunes are in duple meter and 19 in triple. The keys with nos. of tunes are A minor (11), G major (10), C major (7), D major (7), F major (2), A major (1), D minor (1), E minor (1), G minor (2).

tury poets the authorship of many hymns beloved by all church people of whatever denomination: Phoebe Cary ("One sweetly solemn thought"), John G. Whittier ("We may not climb the Heavenly Steeps"), Ray Palmer ("My faith looks up to Thee"), Washington Gladden ("O Master let me walk with Thee"), Phillips Brooks ("O Little Town of Bethlehem"), William Cullen Bryant ("O North, with all thy vales of green!"), Samuel Longfellow ("Holy Spirit, truth divine"), these among many may be cited. Whitley, a sympathetic English observer, interestingly adds:[171] "New England made its own contribution to hymns between 1816 and 1850, chiefly by Unitarians and Congregationalists. The new departure began with Henry Ware of Cambridge; most of his hymns were for special occasions, but his Easter song, 'Lift your glad voices in triumph on high' has become well known. He edited the *Christian Disciple*, whose columns made many writers known, notably Andrews Norton. Of the same school was John Pierpont, whose ode at the opening of a church at Salem, 'O Thou to whom in ancient time' is the best known in England of many written in America. From such men the torch was handed to a new generation. E. H. Sears in 1835 wrote the great carol, 'Calm on the listening ear of night' and fourteen years later matched it with 'It came upon the midnight clear'. Meantime Oliver Wendell Holmes had written 'Lord of all being throned afar'. Later Fanny Crosby contributed two thousand hymns."

I have pointed out that the Methodist revival in England, in the later eighteenth century, was accompanied by vigorous hymn-singing; that is also true of the Moody and Sankey American revival of 1874-1875. We might well remember that the latter would have been less popularly successful if the former had not taught the value of music as a vital expression of religious emotionalism. Although we look down on Moody and Sankey tunes as of little value, nothing is ever really lost, and it may be that, like the white spirituals of the Southern States, the melodies of the 1874 revivals fill a certain place.[172]

---

[171] Whitley, op. cit., p. 158.

[172] The dislike and even contempt felt for the revival tune and hymn were expressed by Henry Ward Beecher in the lively words, "The tunes which burden our modern books by hundreds and thousands, utterly devoid of character, without meaning or substance, may be sung a hundred times and not a person in the con-

The Foundery Collection was not without an influence on American psalmody which may be divided into (a) general and (b) specific or direct. In England the loosening up in rhythm and style appealed to the public, both Independent and Church, though the results came sooner, were more positive, particularly in the former (through the Methodist musical movement) than in the latter. The freedom sought in style and liveliness naturally resulted in license, and later on there was a reaction; still, much may be said in favor of the revival in hymn-singing and the music to which it spontaneously gave birth. This liveliness had its influence indirectly on American psalmody; for the collections of Flagg (1764), James Lyon (*Urania*, 1761), William Billings (1770-1794), Oliver Holden (1792-1803) and many others, either borrowed directly from English collections by Tans'ur, A. and T. Williams, Madan, Milgrove, Rippon, or from the collections *Harmonia Sacra* and *Divine Musical Miscellany*; or copied their salient features, usually doing this without any effect on the correctness of their own compositions.

Perhaps an examination of Samuel Holyoke's very large collection *Columbian Repository* (1802) will prove interesting.[173] Of its 734 tunes 238, or thirty-two per cent, are definitely taken from English sources, Doctor Arne, Doctor Arnold, Doctor Boyce, R. Broderip, Doctor Burney, Calcott, Chetham, Courtville, Darwell, German (3), Handel (10). *Harmonia Sacra*, Doctor Jackson, *Knibb's Collection*, Doctor Madan, Milgrove, Doctor Miller, Doctor Pepusch, Playford, Pleyel, Purcell, Doctor Randall, Shrubsole, Tans'ur, A. Williams, and T. Williams. Holyoke loaded the *Columbian Repository* with 346 tunes out of a total of 734 characterized as "first time anywhere." In the nature of the case I assume these to be composed by Americans, that is, forty-seven per cent of the book, leaving twenty-one per cent unclassified. If, to the collections named above, we add *Este*, the *Genevan* and *English Psalters*, the *Scottish Metrical Psalter* (1635), *Ravenscroft* (1621), and *Playford* (1677) we have specified the main sources of the Colonial hymn tunes.

---

gregation will remember them, there is nothing to remember; they are the very emptiness of fluid noise." Whitley, op. cit.

[173] See pp. 61-62.

Excluding the common and proper tunes from our survey we note that with some exceptions[174] the longer psalm tunes did not appear in the Colonial collections. There has been a revival of interest in them, however, and I give a few references to English and American hymnals.[175]

The Reverend W. H. Havergal, writing in 1850,[176] has all praise for the old tunes in the style of *Dundee, St. Ann, Old Ten Commandments,*[177] *Old 81st, Old 104th*; he says, "The distinctive character of old tunes has long been out of common recollection." He is writing in 1850. "In some respects that character is unsuited to present times. In others it forms the only suitable style for large and mixed congregations. Simple and easy in their phrases and always syllabic in their partition, the commonest ears and least cultivated voices could master them. They are never vulgar, insipid or boisterous. All persons of sober taste and devout feelings delight in them." Havergal believes that singers formerly sang with good speed; a dozen verses, reduced to six by a double tune, formed a very moderate portion for one occasion. When syllabic tunes were introduced in the eighteenth century a slowness of performance necessarily followed. Doctor Watts (d. 1748) complained of the slow singing into which most congregations in his day had fallen; he wanted more speed and a greater care in enunciation.

It may be that the common notion that psalm-singing was doleful, lugubrious, is far from justly founded.

Minor Tunes and Tunes in Triple Time

Students of the seventeenth and eighteenth century psalm-tunes, whether English or American, will be impressed by the large proportion of tunes in minor keys, and in triple time.

Horatio Parker, compiler and editor of *The Hymnal* (1903), now out of print, deprecated the falling-out of the hymn tunes in

---

[174] See Lyon's *Urania*, pp. 40-88.

[175] *Hymns Ancient and Modern,* hist. edn., nos., 174, 400, 334, 621, 217, 316, 193, 371, 335, 230, 503, 386, 340, 517. *The Church Hymnary,* nos. 586, 486, 583, 530, 355, 30, 643. *Songs of Praise,* nos. 43, 176, 195, 693, 655, 216, 443, 211, 512, 191, 615, 329, 197, 526. *Hymns Ancient and Modern,* 1861 edn., nos. 193, 156, 167, 263, 124.

[176] *Old Church Psalmody* by Rev. W. H. Havergal, M. A., Rector of St. Nicholas and honorary Canon of the Cathedral, Worcester, 2nd ed., J. Hart, London, octavo oblong, pp. 72.

[177] See *English Hymnal,* 277; *Church Hymnary,* 289.

minor keys from the repertory of the ordinary congregation. American congregations as a rule do not seem to care for the minor key, and in consequence our American hymnals have a smaller proportion of such tunes than have the hymnals for England. The truth of that will be patent to anyone who will take the trouble to make an actual count of the tunes in any of the leading collections in Great Britain and the United States. The table below will express by percentages the relative proportions of major and minor pieces, and of duple or triple times used. The percentages illustrate graphically certain tendencies in New England psalmody. As time went on minor tunes were used less and less and the more demonstrative triple time tunes were not so favored.[178] The analysis of the collections has seldom extended to the whole of it, but in all cases a fairly representative section has been taken. Altogether over 1400 tunes were observed.

TABLE

Name of Collection.	TUNES		TIMES	
	Maj.	Min.	Dup.	Tri.
1621 *Ravenscroft, Th.*	49	38	—	—
1726 Tufts's *Introduction*	54	46	73	27
1765 *Tate & Brady Supplement*	59	41	—	—
1766 *Bayley's Walter's Grounds*	61	39	40	60
1782 *Chorister's Companion*	54	46	65	35
1793 *Rural Harmony*	75	25	—	—
1804 *Bridgewater Collection, Second Edition*	73	27	70	30
1806 *Salem Collection*	80	20	45	55
1807 *Newburyport Collection*	68	32	65	15
1807 *Massachusetts Collection of Sacred Harmony*	65	35	—	—
1808 *Columbian Sacred Harmonist*	77	23	67	33
1816 *New York Selection of Sacred Music*	73	27	52	48
1818 *Laus Deo* (Jenks)	64	36	61	39
1820 *Bridgewater Collection Eighth Edition*	80	20	—	—

[178] At the present time, however, there is a marked tendency on the part of American hymn-book compilers to follow the lead of *Hymns Ancient and Modern*, the *English Hymnal*, the new *Methodist* and *Baptist Hymnals*, and the *Church Hymnary*, by including a considerable proportion of tunes in minor keys. A conspicuous instance of this is *Hymns of the Spirit for Use in the Free Churches of America*, The Beacon Press, Inc., Boston 1937. Nine per cent of the tunes are minor.

CHAPTER TWENTY

Experiments in Musical Notation

In 1563 John Day published *The Whole Psalmes in foure Partes*, with a frontispiece showing a gentleman of severe aspect confronting a lady, presumably his wife, who is attended by her children. The gentleman has the forefinger of his left hand resting confidingly, yet peremptorily, on the thumb of his right hand. This, I presume, is intended to show the father of a family in the act of instructing his family in music through the help of the Guidonian Hand.[179] Just as the abacus was evolved from the ten fingers of two hands, so did Guido of Arezzo (b. 995) turn to the hand as a help in teaching the cumbrous mediaeval notation of music.

The ingenuity of the American composer did not find entire satisfaction in composing 'fuguing'-tunes, but was diverted occasionally into inventing new forms of musical notation; these new forms were always so logical and so saving of time in study or expense in printing that their authors did not hesitate to scrap ruthlessly the five-line staff with all its accoutrements, the result of several centuries of development. We need not spend much time with these experimental notations. One of the first to come to notice in New England is that of the Reverend John Tufts; it consisted simply of the first letter of the syllable used in solemization, placed on the proper line or space of the staff, with lateral dots to show notes of varied lengths.[180] This was anticipated in part by the device used in the *Sternhold & Hopkins Psalter* (1594), printed by John Windet and referred to in the chapter, "The Rhythm and Meter of the Reformation Psalters."

The Reverend Andrew Law was born in Connecticut and educated in Brown University, but practiced the art of music teach-

---

[179] See Appendix N. Also Dr. Scholes, *Puritans and Music*, p. 272.
[180] Metcalf, op. cit., gives an illustration, p. 18.

ing mainly in or about Philadelphia; Metcalf gives an excellent account of his career.[181] In 1803 he published *The Musical Primer*, adding stems or filling in the heads or adding 'flags' to stems to take care of their relative lengths; it will be noted that Law had dispensed with the staff quite light-heartedly. Though not followed closely in details he had imitators as regards 'shaped notes.'[182] Perhaps as pathetic as any of these experiments in reforming our musical notation is that outlined in the *Christian Minstrel* (1851, twentieth edition); evidently a popular collection. In this notation, although the key of the music is stated, it is always written as if in the key of C. The Christian minstrels were thus able to rid themselves of all that nonsense of sharp or flat key-signatures.

We get a side light on the practical side of the notation when we read the following from page 1 of *Carmina Sacra*, by Lowell Mason and T. B. Mason (1852), viz.: "The proprietors of *'Mason's Sacred Harp'* have (contrary to the express wishes and views of the authors) stereotyped a volume of this work in Patent Notes, in belief that it would be more acceptable to singers in the West and South, where Patent Notes are more extensively used."

The allusion to patent notes brings up the whole question as to the origin of what I have disrespectfully called a freak notation, a question which is outside the scope of this book, but may yet claim a little attention on two grounds, (a) as showing the development of the 'shaped' or patent note idea, and (b) as drawing attention to the valuable work by George Pullen Jackson, *White Spirituals in the Southern Uplands*.[183] Doctor Jackson and others whom he names have recognized the spirituals of the white people as a type in folk song, but many students of cultural phenomena have shied from these religious folk songs in the belief that they are linked up with 'psalmody' or 'hymnody,' and hence not a part of folklore at all, not important or even interesting. Then, too, those who have felt the value of the white spirituals have lacked

---

[181] Op. cit., pp. 69-79, with illustration of his notation with varied shapes for note-heads.

[182] John Wyeth, *Depository of Sacred Music* (1826); Allen D. Garden, *The Missouri Harmony* (1831); Snyder & Chapell, *The Western Lyre* (1831); William Walker, *The Southern Harmony* (1850).

[183] University of North Carolina Press, 1933; p. 25 gives a valuable list of 38 collections using 'shaped-notes.'

material for their study. Doctor Jackson begins his book with a sketch of New England psalmody from the collections of John Tufts and Thomas Walter down to the publication in 1798 of *The Easy Instructor*, at this point the genealogical tree of the 'fasola' books i.e., books using 'shaped notes' branched off from what may be called the main art stem; Doctor Jackson considers that William Little and William Smith and not Andrew Law, were the real originators of the patent notes; I presume this opinion must be taken as final.[184]

In reading Doctor Jackson's informing study of the 'fasola folk' living in the hills, high valleys, and mountains of the Southern States, we become aware of an extensive song-literature written and composed by them. A musician must examine this music before he can understand what it offers to the people who practice and love it. I have found the *Original Sacred Harp*[185] most helpful in learning this. Although the preface on the rudiments of music contains the usual cautions as to consecutives, the pages are peppered and salted with them. The tunes often have a pentatonic flavor and invariably a pleasing lilt. There is very little modulation, though the minor tunes slip easily into the relative major. Occasionally the 7th sound in minor has its accidental, but usually it is printed as a flat 7th. Along these limits the music shows much invention.

---

[184] *The Easy Instructor*, William Smith, Albany, N. Y., probably the 4th edn., is in the Massachusetts Historical Society Library. *Ecclesiae Harmonia*, Charles Woodward, 2nd edn., 1809—curious, even fantastic notation, is seen in No. 972—in the Lowell Mason Library, Yale University.

[185] *Original Sacred Harp* (Denson revision), copyright, 1936, and published by the Sacred Harp Publishing Company, Inc., Haleyville, Alabama. Oblong, 9½ by 7, 460 pp.

CHAPTER TWENTY-ONE

The New Era

It is plain that the New England composers, whether from a hardly excusable ignorance or from deliberate choice, had excluded themselves from the main musical currents and from artistic fellowship with their English cousins. The inevitable followed. Sonneck[186] describes how "the influx (1790) of skilled European composers, destined to revolutionize our musical life, mainly to its advantage (but in certain respects to our disadvantage), widened into an ever-broadening stream. That such men as Reinagle, Hewitt, B. Carr, Taylor, who brought with them a knowledge of the best music of their age, did not take friendly to the crudities of Billings and other early church composers, goes without saying."

General social and political conditions at the close of the eighteenth century were such as to stimulate progressive ideas not only in business but in government, education and the arts. In 1789 the national constitution was adopted; George Washington, John Adams, Thomas Jefferson, and Alexander Hamilton were active; the war of 1812, ending satisfactorily for the Americans, had intensified national feeling. The time was now ripe, among other things, for a new and better music; "the aesthetic interests of the American colonists, like those of the intellect, were subject to the law of inheritance, the demands of the local environment, the process of change, and the impacts from outside."[187] Billings's last work had been published in 1794; the *Massachusetts Compiler* (1795) had indirectly given a blow to the older music by its compliance with the demands of musical correctness ignored by Billings and his followers; in 1792 Lowell Mason's birth had been recorded in Medfield, Massachusetts; in 1802 the *Columbian Re-*

---

[186] Op. cit.
[187] *Rise of American Civilization*, Charles A. and Mary R. Beard.

pository of Sacred Harmony, the largest one-volume collection of the Colonial period, was published by Samuel Holyoke; the *Salem Collection of Classical Sacred Music* appeared in 1805; the Boston Handel and Haydn Society began its long and honorable career in 1815, publishing its own collection of music in 1822. These various happenings gave the first ten or twenty years of the nineteenth century a character all its own: it was a record of a protest and a hope, in short the beginning of a new era.

It is worth while to record here the more noteworthy of the protests against the Billings school of writing hymn-tunes. One of the earliest of these is the part Oliver Holden took in publishing the *Massachusetts Compiler*, coöperating with Samuel Holyoke, the Harvard graduate, and Hans Gram, the professional musician. Holden, although nineteen years younger than Billings, up to the time the *Massachusetts Compiler* appeared may be considered to belong to the Billings school; Holyoke and Gram were definitely, by training and predilection, opposed to it. It may be that Holden, being a man of affairs, was persuaded by the two (for their evident advantage) to join hands with them, or perhaps Holden, owing to the popularity of *Coronation*, had realized that he might stand in his own shoes. Much of his work however ('fuguing' tunes, for example) stamps him as a Billings man. Although at his best he was never as lively rhythmically as the older man, he had a feeling for harmony and phrase-balance. At any rate, the inclusion of Holden in the anti-Billings campaign was significant.

Other significant gestures in favor of correct harmony managed in accordance with the English practice of Tans'ur and Williams were (a) the protests of the *Salem Collection of Classical Sacred Music*,[188] (b) the preface to the first edition of the Boston *Handel and Haydn Society Collection*,[189] (c) the irenic preface to *Songs of Zion* by the compiler and composer, Reverend Thomas Whittemore.[190]

---

[188] 1805, no editor named.

[189] 1822, admitting alterations of the old tunes but promising to retain (in general) the airs of the several tunes unaltered.

[190] 1836, Whittemore (1800-1861) included 21 of the 'ancient' tunes in his collection, but states that he made 'absolutely unavoidable alterations in them.' His own tunes show him to have been a schooled musician. He condemns banishing the 'ancient' tunes from the modern books.

But the old tunes, with all their charged faults, did not lack for stout defenders. The corrections of the errors in harmony by the new school inspired resentment in the hearts of the old-timers. In 1836 the *Billings and Holden Collection of Ancient Psalmody*,[191] under the patronage of the Boston Billings and Holden Society was issued under a plea that "these tunes must be republished as originally written, or the elderly and middle-aged will be deprived of the satisfaction and delight they have heretofore experienced." This was certainly a mild, even pathetic remonstrance.

We need a Greek chorus at this point with its interpretative voice to sound a peaceful note: "Let the old fellows alone; they meant well and filled a place in their day. If one doesn't care for the old tunes, peppered and salted with musical blunders, one is not obliged to sing them!"

LOWELL MASON

At this day it is seen that the compiler and editor of the *Handel and Haydn Society Collection* (1822), Lowell Mason (1792-1872), was the protagonist of the new era in music. His work in compiling this collection had made him acquainted with the better kinds of choral music used in English and German churches; the very title of the new collection indicates clearly the sources of his ideals.

Although now acknowledged to have been the man for the hour, to have had a love for music genuine and unselfish, and to have used his leadership with wisdom and fidelity to high ideals of public service, no authoritative life of Lowell Mason is available[192] (1939). Metcalf gives an excellent sketch, which should be read in connection with the discriminating estimate of Mason's relations to the old and new eras, given by Professor Waldo Selden Pratt.[193]

The main facts of Lowell Mason's life are that he was born in Medfield, Massachusetts, a small town about fifteen miles from

---

[191] There were 304 pp.; the 'ancient' composers reprinted (with the nos. of their tunes) were Billings (40), Holden (28), Holyoke (2), Swan (6), Belknap (6), Kimball (6), French (3), Bartholemew Brown (2), Holt (2), Read (8).

[192] It is hoped that a biography by his grandson, Henry L. Mason, in preparation for several years, will soon appear.

[193] Metcalf, op. cit., pp. 211-216; Grove *American Supplement*, article "Lowell Mason."

Boston. He must have been of a studious disposition and with a natural bent towards writing, for when he offered the *Handel and Haydn Society Collection* to the Boston people he was only thirty; his travels in Europe and his association with George James Webb[194] the Englishman whose musical knowledge and culture must have been indispensable to him in the development of his ideas, came later. From 1827 to 1832 Mason was president of the Handel and Haydn Society, and was instrumental in founding the Boston Academy of Music in 1832, in which he and Webb were professors.

It is possible that our greatest indebtedness to Lowell Mason arises from his unceasing energy in the cause of music for the people, especially public school music; his publications in this latter field were numerous. In 1838 he became the director of music in the schools of Boston. New York University (1855) gave him the degree of Doctor of Music. As a composer his name is familiar in America and in Great Britain as the author of many popular hymn-tunes, particularly *Missionary Hymn*,[195] *Hamburg, Olivet, Bethany, Boylston, Antioch*. He was interested in making arrangements from Gregorian or other melodies to be used as hymn-tunes. Mason did not always claim authorship for his tunes, but it is probable that their number, excluding arrangements, is over 150, and possibly nearer 200.

Binney's *Congregational Church Music* (1853)[196] is interesting as introducing Lowell Mason in connection with English psalmody. "His tunes had a long run of popularity, especially among Non-conformists and are not likely to be soon forgotten, if only modern editors will leave the original but effective harmonies alone."[197]

The new era, which I have with reason, I believe, dated as beginning with the publication of the *Handel and Haydn Society Collection* (1822) was not a very fruitful era; a great deal of

---

[194] B. Salisbury, England, 1803, went to the U. S. in 1830, d. in Orange, N. J., in 1887.

[195] This is the only tune by an American that is found in the better English Hymnals, e.g. *Church Hymns*, edited by Arthur Sullivan (1874); *Bristol Tune Book* (1881); *Worship Music* (1905); *Hymns Ancient and Modern* (1909 and 1924); *Baptist Hymnal* (1933); *English Hymnal* (1933); and *Methodist Hymnbook* (1933). Other references are possible.

[196] Lightwood, op. cit., p. 294.

[197] See Appendix O.

music was printed, many collections in the familiar oblong format appeared, made by industrious music teachers; but it was not until the convulsion of the War between the States came that the people were ready again for newer and better things in church music. The significant names of the new dispensation heroes are Dudley Buck (March 10, 1839-October 6, 1909), John K. Paine (January 9, 1839-April 25, 1906), and James C. D. Parker (June 2, 1828-November 27, 1916). The periods of their American activity began respectively in 1862, 1862, 1854. It remains for someone to cover the fifty years from 1820 to 1870 with a purpose of showing what was done, how it was done, and what its worth was, particularly making plain the relationship of Buck, Paine and Parker to the years following as well as to those preceding them.

APPENDIX

APPENDIX A

Winchester Old (Este, 1592): analysis of harmony

The analysis is founded on Rimbault's edition of Este's *Whole Book of Psalms* (1592). For simplicity's sake the Rimbault score of four lines with G, C, and F clefs is reduced to two lines with G and F clefs. The tune is *Winchester,* one of the five tunes in *Este* having a place-name. (The tune is often called *Winchester Old.*)

The music is noted as in four phrases, the air being in the tenor. The two final chords in each phrase may be looked upon as cadential chords, the keys indicated being respectively G minor (half close), C major (full close), D minor (half close), F major (full close). The phrases all begin on a longer note.

Of the 28 chords in the tune 25 have their roots and 3, their third in the bass; there are no chords with their fifth in the bass. In other words the harmony has great simplicity with much strength.

The following appeared first in Este's *Whole Book of Psalms* (1592), set to Psalm 84:

How pleas-ant is thy dwell-ing place O Lord of hosts to me

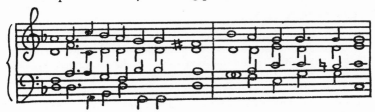

The tab-er-na-cles of thy grace How pleas-ant, Lord, they be

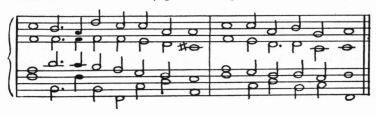

APPENDIX B

Singing by rule

A Sketch/of/the History/of/Newbury, Newburyport, and West Newton/from 1626 to 1843/by Joshua Coffin, A.B.S. H.C. Boston 1717. Pp. 414.

Coffin writes:

"In this year[a] the reverend John Tufts, of the west parish published a small work on music, entitled, 'A very plain and easy introduction to the art of singing psalm-tunes, with the cantus or treble of twenty-eight psalm-tunes in such a manner as that the learner may attain the skill of singing them with the greatest ease and speed imaginable, by the reverend Mr. John Tufts. Price six pence or five shillings per dozen.' Small as this book must have been to be afforded for six pence per copy it was at this time a great novelty it being the first publication of the kind in New England if not in America. As late as 1700 there were not more than four or five tunes known in many of the congregations in the country, and in some not more than two or three, and even these sung altogether by rote. These tunes were *York, Hackney, Saint Mary's, Windsor* and *Martyrs.* To publish at this time a book on music containing the enormous number of twenty-eight psalm-tunes in three parts and wholly choral, although it was only a reprint of Ravenscroft which was first published in 1618[b] was an innovation on the old, time-honored customs of the country and the attempt to teach singing by note thus commenced by Mr. Tufts was most strenuously resisted by that large class of persons everywhere to be found who believe that an old error is better than a new truth. Many at that time imagined that *fa, sol, la* was in reality nothing but popery in disguise. A writer in the New England Chronicle in 1723[e] thus observes, 'Truly, I have a great jealousy that if we once begin to sing by rule the next thing which be to pray by rule and preach by rule and *then comes popery.*' "

Coffin goes on to say:[d]

"In 1721 reverend Thomas Walter of Roxbury published a book on music entitled 'the grounds and rules of music explained or an introduction to the singing by note fitted to the meanest capacity.' In the preface Mr. Walter writes, 'The tunes now in use in our churches when they came out of the hands of the composers of them were sung according to the rules of the scale of musick, but are now miserably tortured and twisted and quavered in some churches into a horrid medley of confused and disorderly noises. Our tunes for want of a standard to appeal to in our singing, left to the mercy of every un-skilful throat to chap and alter, twist and change according to their infinitely divers and no less od humours and fancies. No two churches sing alike. At present we are confined to eight or ten tunes, and in some congregations to little more than half that number.' "

---

[a] 1714, p. 185.
[b] An examination of *Ravenscroft*, first published in 1621, will show that Tufts did not derive from him.
[e] See *New England Chronicle.*
[d] Op. cit., p. 186.

APPENDIX C

Tunes from Ainsworth, The Bay Psalm Book, Tufts, and Walter in modern hymnals

Psalm-tunes in the four early New England collections, viz. Ainsworth's *The Book of Psalms,* 1612), the *Bay Psalm Book* (1698), the Reverend Walter's *Grounds and Rules* (1721), and the Reverend Tufts's *Introduction to the Singing of Psalms* (1726), with date of first appearance,—first and second phrases only.

Reference letters: *Ainsworth,* A. *Bay Psalm Book,* B. *Walter,* W. *Tufts,* T.*

The name or letter at the end of the line to the right gives the author or collection from which the music is taken.

Of these tunes many are found in modern hymnals; a representative group of English, Scottish, and American collections has been searched and appearances of any of these old tunes recorded.

Reference letters:

CH *The Church Hymnary* with supplement, 1930, Oxford University Press.
EH *The English Hymnal* with tunes, 1933, Humphrey Milford.
HAM *Hymns Ancient and Modern,* 1924, London, William Clowes and Son, Ltd.
Hist. Ed. *Hymns Ancient and Modern,* historical edition, 1909.
IE *In Excelsis,* 1911, New York, The Century Company.
MH *The Methodist Hymn-book,* 1933, London, Methodist Conference Office.
NH *The New Hymnal,* 1916, authority of the Protestant Episcopal Church.
PH *The Pilgrim Hymnal,* 1931, Boston, The Pilgrim Press.
SP *The Scottish Psalter,* 1929, Oxford University Press.
TH *The Hymnal,* 1934, New York.

---

* No. 557 in H. A. and M. (1924) is a version in duple meter of the Old 81st.

THE TUNES

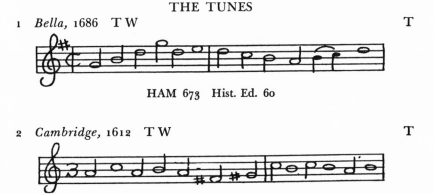

1 *Bella,* 1686 T W   T

HAM 673 Hist. Ed. 60

2 *Cambridge,* 1612 T W   T

153

3 *Canterbury,* 1592 B T W   T

4 *Commandments,* 1556 A T W   T

CH 305 (1549) HAM 201 (1547) Hist. Ed. 336 SP 6 (1549)

5 *Exeter,* 1623 T   T

(First two phrases like St. Matthias)

6 *Gloucester,* 1621 T W   T

7 *Hackneys (St. Mary's),* 1621 B T W   T

CH 401 EH 84 HAM 93 Hist. Ed. 103

8 *Hanover,* 1708 T   Croft or Handel

CH 9 EH 466 HAM 431 Hist. Ed. 326 (1708) IE 7 MH 8 NH 255
PH 144 TH 2

9 *Isle of Wight* T (Sometimes *"Isle of White"*)   T

154

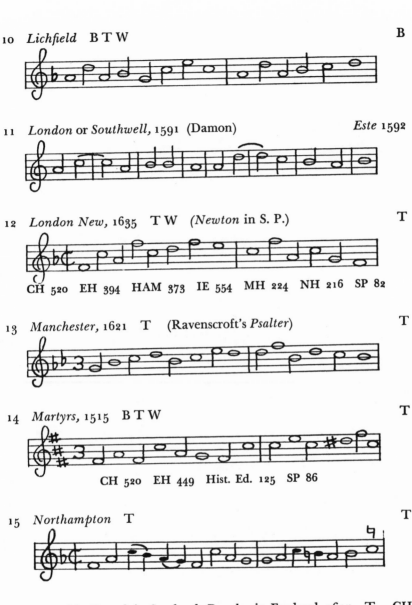

10 *Lichfield* B T W   B

11 *London* or *Southwell,* 1591 (Damon)   *Este* 1592

12 *London New,* 1635 T W *(Newton* in S. P.)   T

CH 520 EH 394 HAM 373 IE 554 MH 224 NH 216 SP 82

13 *Manchester,* 1621 T (Ravenscroft's *Psalter*)   T

14 *Martyrs,* 1515 B T W   T

CH 520 EH 449 Hist. Ed. 125 SP 86

15 *Northampton* T   T

16 *Norwich, French* in Scotland, *Dundee* in England, 1615 T CH

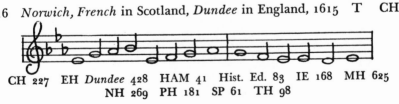

CH 227 EH *Dundee* 428 HAM 41 Hist. Ed. 83 IE 168 MH 625
NH 269 PH 181 SP 61 TH 98

155

17 *Oxford,* 1621   B T W   T

18 *Penetential Hymn*   A T W   T

19 *Peterborough*   T W   T

20 *Portsmouth* or *Nemur*   T W   T

See note to Psalm 113.

21 *Psalm 18,* 1561   T   T

CH 586   SP 149

22 *Psalm 81,* 1564   A T W   (1592 in *Este*) see footnote *e*   T

CH 355 (1562)   EH 461   HAM 439 (1562)   Hist. Ed. 217   SP 154

23 *Psalm 100,* 1551   A B T W   T

CH 229   EH 365   HAM 166   Hist. Ed. 316   IE 1   MH 2   NH 249
PH 9   SP 13   TH 1

156

24 *Psalm 112*, 1537 A T W (known also as *Vater unser*) T

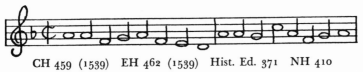

CH 459 (1539) EH 462 (1539) Hist. Ed. 371 NH 410

25 *Psalm 113*, 1525 numbered 115 in *Bay Psalm-Book* A B T W T

CH 217 EH 544 HAM 171 Hist. Ed. 335 MH 584

The natural in the first phrase was a common error in early collections. *Ravenscroft* (1621), however, has the B flat. This air is taken from the *Genevan Psalter* of 1539, and also of 1562, for Psalm 36; in 1562 it also is set for Psalm 68. In the *Anglo-Genevan Psalter* of 1561 it was set to Psalm 113 and became the "Old 113th." In the *Genevan Psalter*, Psalm 68 became known as the battle song of the Huguenots. See *Musical Times*, London, 1881, p. 555, and *Handbook to the Church Hymnary*, p. 78.

The authorship of the music is in doubt.

26 *Psalm 115*, see *Psalm 113*

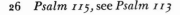

27 *Psalm 119*, 1560 A B T W T

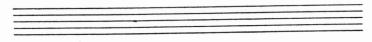

28 *Psalm 148*, 1635 A B T W B

29 *Psalm 149* or *Hanover*, 1708 T W

CH 9 EH 466 HAM 431 Hist. Ed. 326 IE 7 PH 144

30 *Sabbath Hymn* T   T

31 *St. David's*, 1621 B T W   T

CH 31 EH 166 HAM 352 Hist. Ed. 542 MH 721 SP 103

32 *St. James'*, 1697 T W   T

CH 173 EH 341 HAM 199 Hist. Ed. 344 MH 575 N 279 SP 110

33 *St. Mary's*, see *Hackney*

34 *St. Matthias*, 1623 (Orlando Gibbons)   O. Gibbons

CH 433 HAM 549 Hist. Ed. 450 SP 116

35 *Southwell*, 1591 (Damon) A B T W   T

In B, *Cambridge Short Tune;* sometimes called *London Old*   Hist. Ed. 462

36 *Southwell*, 1579 (Damon)   Hist. Ed.

CH 102 EH 77 HAM 120 Hist. Ed. 354 MH 239

158

37 *Standish* T W   T

38 *Vater unser,* 1537   A T W   T

(Psalm 112, q.v.)

39 *Veni Creator,* 1592   T   T

40 *Walsal,* 1721   T

CH 148   EH 13   HAM 633   Hist. Ed. 294   MH 281   NH 496
SP 139 (1720)

41 *Westminster* T W   T

42 *Windsor, Dundee* in Scotland, 1591 (Damon)   A B T W   T

CH 276 *Dundee*   EH 332   HAM 267   Hist. Ed. 97   IE 280   MH 625
NH 124   PH 50   SP 51 (*Dundee*)

43 *Worcester* T   T

159

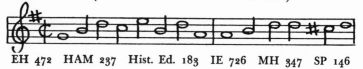

EH 472   HAM 237   Hist. Ed. 183   IE 726   MH 347   SP 146

APPENDIX D

James Lyon respects Billings's music

The inclusion of a composer outside the geographical domain of the New England psalmodists may seem incompatible with the plan of this book. We ought, however, to take into account the importance of Lyon's *Urania,* the interest which Billings's music excited in Philadelphia and such significant facts as the inclusion by Lyon in a programme of his own *Let the shrill trumpet's martial voice* and *The Lord descended from above* with Billings's *The rose of Sharon and the lily of the vallies.* Lyon may be justly considered a part of a movement beginning in New England and in contact with it by reason of his evident respect for Billings's music.

APPENDIX E

Billings's burial place

In a letter to William H. Capen of Stoughton, Massachusetts,* an authority on William Billings, the City Clerk of Boston writes:

"The name of William Billings was carried in the Boston Directory of 1796 and 1798 as a singing master at 89 Newbury Street. His name does not appear in the list of those who suffered loss by the fire of 1794, and there is no record that Billings was ever granted permission to construct a tomb in any of the burying-grounds."

This appears to be all the information we have in the records concerning William Billings; it seems to be of little or no value in clearing up the question of his burial-place.

See also Metcalf, op. cit., p. 55.

APPENDIX F

Billings finds difficulties in book publishing

"This work is a part of the Book of Anthems which I have so long promised; my reasons for not publishing the whole in one Volume must

---

* Deceased.

be obvious to all who consider the present extraordinary price of Copper-plate and Paper; the Copper in special is so fearse that I don't think it possible to procure enough to contain the Whole at any Price; besides if I was able to publishe the Whole, but few would become purchasers and I believe that most will be of my opinion, when I inform them the book could not be afforded for less than Ten Dollars. However I hope that notwithstanding the present Difficulties I shall shortly be able to publish Remainder at a much lower price."

Psalm Singers' Amusement

APPENDIX G

The nature of Billings's power

There is abundance of material in proof that Billings was a natural melodist. He had no constructive powers, it is true; that is another matter. His feeling for the proper adaptation of the musical rhythm to the poetical meter was also at times ludicrously lacking. But he did have a strong sense of the power of music as regards expressing grandeur, intense feeling, and pathos; if he had been born fifty years later than 1746 he would have been a notable figure in our national music.

APPENDIX H

237 *Billings's tunes*

Names of William Billings's tunes, with the name of the collection in which they made their first appearance: *A. New England Psalm-Singer. B. Singing Master's Assistant. C. Music in Miniature. D. Psalm Singer's Amusement. E. Suffolk Harmony. F. Continental Harmony.* *Stoughton Music Society Centennial Collection, 1878.*

Adams F*	Baltimore B	Brattle Street F
Adoration D	Bangor C	Brest C
Africa A	Baptism E	Bridgewater A
Albany A	Barre A	Broad Cove F
America A	Bellingham F	Buckingham C
Amherst A	Beneficence E	Burlington E
Andover A	Benevolence B	Brookfield A*
Ashford A	Berlin D*	Brookline A
Ashham B	Bethlehem B	Brunswick B
Asia A	Bolton B	Calvary C
Assurance D	Boston A	Cambridge A
Attleborough A	Braintree A	Camden E
Aurora B*	Brattle Square E	Charlestown A

Chelsea A
Chester A*
Chesterfield A
Chocksett B
Claremont F
Cobham F
Cohassett F
Columbia B
Concord A
Connection B
Conquest E
Consolation B
Corsica A
Creation C*
Cross Street F
Crucifixion C
Cumberland A
Danbury B
David's Lamentation B*
Dedham A
Dickinson A
Delaware C
Dighton A
Dorchester A
Dublin C
Dudley C
Dunstable B
Duxborough A
Eastham A
East Sudbury F
East Town A
Eden E
Egypt F
Eighteenth Psalm A
Election E
Emanuel D*
Emmaus B
Essex A
Europe A
Exeter B
Fairfield A
Fitchburg C
Framingham C
Franklin C
Freedom A
Friendship A
Georgia A
Gilead F
Gloucester E

Golgotha D*
Great Plain F
Greenland A
Halifax B
Hampshire A
Hampton A
Hanover A
Hanover New A
Hartford D
Harvard A
Haverhill A
Heath B
Hebron A
Hingham A
Holden A
Hollis A
Hollis Street A
Hopkinton F*
Hull E
Invocation F
Ipswich A
Isle of White C
Jamaica A
Jargon B
Jerusalem E
Jordan E*
Judea B
Lancaster A
Lebanon A*
Lewis Town F
Lexington A
Liberty A
Lincoln A
Lynn A
Madrid C
Majesty B*
Malden A
Manchester B
Mansfield C
Marshfield A
Maryland B*
Massachusetts A
Medfield A
Medford A
Medway B
Mendom D
Middlesex A
Middletown A
Milton A

Modern Music D
Moravia E
Morning Hymn F
Morpheus C
Nantasket A
Nantucket A
Nazareth C
Newburn C
New Castle C
New Colchester C
New Hingham A
New North A
New Plymouth F
Newport A
New South A
Newtown A
Norfolk F
Northborough E
North Providence B
North River A
Nutfield A
Old Brick A
Old North A
Old South A
Orange Street A
Orleans A
Oxford C
Paris C*
Pembroke A
Pembroke New A
Petersburg E
Philadelphia B
Philanthropy E
Phoebus B*
Pitt A
Plainfield A
Pleasant Street A
Plymton A
Pomfret A
Portsmouth C
Pownall A
Princetown A
Providence A
Pumpily A
Purchase Street A
Putney C
Queen Street A
Redemption D
Resignation D

Restoration E
Resurrection E
Revelation C
Richmond B
Rochester F
Rocky Nook F
Roxbury A
Royalston C
Rutland D
Saint Andrews F
Saint Elisha A
Saint Enoch F
Saint Hellen's C
Saint Johns F
Sappho B*
Savannah B
Saybrook C
Scituate A
Sharon B
Sherburne B

Shiloh E
Shirley A
Sinai E
Smithfield A
South Boston F
Spain B
Stockbridge B*
Stoughton A
Sturbridge C
Sudbury A*
Suffolk A
Sullivan B
Summer Street A
Sunday B
Swanzey A
Taunton A
Thomas-Town F
Tower Hill A
Trinity New C
Unity A

Union A
Vermont B
Victory F
Waltham B
Wareham C
Warren B
Washington B
Washington Street F
Watertown A
Wellfleet A
West
West Boston E
Westfield A
West Sudbury F
Weymouth F
Wheelers Point A
Wilkes A
Williamsburg A
Worcester B
Wrentham B

NOTE: The following tunes by Billings do not appear in either of the above collections: *Antipatris, Best, Connecticut, Kittery, Moriah, New Boston, Number 45, Russia,†* St. *Thomas, Sudbury West, True Penitent, Uxbridge, West, West Johns.*

APPENDIX I

Collections of the 'fasola' or 'shaped-note' singers

Doctor George Pullen Jackson's book, *White Spirituals*, has been a revelation to me (and I imagine to the majority of cultured, concert-going musicians) of the existence of a very large body of musically experienced choral singers living in the Southern and Western States who are following the New England traditions of solmization, and who keep alive, through frequent performances, the works of William Billings, Oliver Holden and others of the Billings school.[1] But these singers themselves write hymn-tunes or transmit by the help of oral tradition many old ones. Many of their pieces are modal and the words they select are usually serious and concerned with life, its sorrows, death and the afterlife.

---

† A tune in the *M. E. Church Hymnal*, 1878, strongly resembling this, is attributed to Daniel Read.

[1] *White Spirituals in the Southern Uplands; the story of the Fasola Folk, their Songs, Singing, and 'Buckwheat Notes.'* George Pullen Jackson. Chapel Hill, the University of North Carolina Press, 1933. Pp. xv-444.

Doctor Jackson (op. cit) gives data of 38 song-books connected with the 'fasola' singers and printed in the 'four-shape' notation. *The Easy Instructor*, by William Little and William Smith, Albany, 1798, is credited by Doctor Jackson as the first of the four-shape notation books.[g] Andrew Law followed in 1803 with *The Art of Singing*, in three parts; Law uses a four-shaped notation, but it is not applied to the staff of five lines, nor is it applied to the major scale in the same way that Little and Smith applied it in 1798.[g] Other books not listed by Doctor Jackson, using a new notation (not necessarily the four-shape) are *Harmonic Companion and Guide to Social Worship*, Andrew Law, 1807;[g] *The New Brunswick Collection*, Van Devanter, 1829;[h] *The Christian Minstrel*, J. B. Aikin, Philadelphia, 1846;[h] *The One Line Psalmist*, H. W. Day, 1849.[h]

APPENDIX J

A help to "perfect solfayeing"

The pages of 'grounds' often found in the psalters just preceding the tunes are sometimes almost pathetic in their desire to help the psalm-singer. A *Sternhold & Hopkins Psalter*, 1594, printed by John Windet for the assignees of Richard Daye (Hartford Seminary Foundation Library) has the following:

"To the Reader: Thou shalt understand (gentle reader) that I have (for the helpe of those that are desirous to learn to sing) caused a new print of note to be made with letters to be joined to every note: whereby thou mayest know how to call every note by his right name, so that with a very little diligence (as thou art taught in this introduction printed heretofore in the Psalmes) thou mayest more easilie by the viewing of these letters, come to the knowledge of perfect solfayeing: whereby thou mayest sing the Psalmes the more speedilie and easilie; the letters be these V for VT, R for Fe, M for My, F for Fa, S for Sol, L for La. Thus where you see any letter joyned by the notes you may easilie call him by his right name, as by these two examples you the better perceive.

Ut   Re   Mi   Fa   Sol   La

Thus I commit thee unto him that liveth forever, who grant that we sing with our hearts unto the glorie of his holy name. A M E N."

---

[g] Massachusetts Historical Society Library.
[h] Lowell Mason Library, Yale University.

APPENDIX K

Josiah Flagg antedates William Billings

William Billings's first collection *The New England Psalm-Singer,* 1770, was antedated by Josiah Flagg's *A Collection of the Best Psalm-Tunes,* 1764. For an interesting and sympathetic account of Flagg see O. G. Sonneck's *Early Concert Life in America,* pp. 261-264.

A Collection of the Best Psalm-Tunes in 2, 3, and 4 parts from the most-approved Authors, Josiah Flagg, Philadelphia, 1764, 67 pp., oblong. (Boston Public Library, 447.18.) The index lists 116 tunes. *Old Hundred* has the melodic variation occasionally heard in the fourth (last) phrase, viz., the four final notes are *mi-fa-re-do. March of Richard III* is probably taken from the *Foundery Tune-Book* (John Wesley), 1742. Many historically important tunes are in the book; there are no Colonial tunes: an interesting collection. It is engraved by Paul Revere.

APPENDIX L

Waldo Selden Pratt's French Psalter of 1562

Just about the time the revision of this appreciation of the New England psalmody and its composers had been completed, Professor Waldo Selden Pratt published his *The Music of the French Psalter of 1562: A historical survey and analysis with the music in modern notation.* Columbia University Press, 1939, Pp. X-213.

This work of Professor Pratt's will most admirably and usefully help the student when used in conjunction with Douen's *Clément Marot* and Henry Expert's assembling of the melodies of the *French Psalter of 1562.* Pratt devotes 130 pages to the melodies and painstakingly analyzes them.

APPENDIX M

Sixteenth century harmony

O. Douen gives a great amount of material for research along harmonic lines.[1] *Chanson spirituelle* by Clément Jannequin (sixteenth century), 95 bars, four voices, employs largely triads in root position, with several instances of first inversions; the second position (six-four chord) is scrupulously avoided, even at cadences, or if used softened by the suspension 4-3; passing and other non-harmonic tones are used freely, parallel fifths and octaves do not occur.

Psalme I by C. Goudimel (1510-1572), 54 bars, four voices, triads in root position and first inversion, one case of the second inversion softened by the 4-3 suspension and context.

---

[1] Douen, op. cit., vol. 2, pp. 78, 120, 197, et seq.

Psalme 104 by C. Goudimel, 172 bars, four voices; there are three cases of second inversions, but in no case at the cadence; suspensions are common; triads are found only in root position and first inversion, except as just stated; four cases of the omission of the triad's third; one case of parallel fifths on unaccented beat; free use of passing tones.

As we go on in Douen with seventeenth century examples, the restrictions to root positions and first inversions of triads, with a steady avoidance of the second inversion especially at the cadence, continue. Passing and other non-harmonic tones are freely used; omissions of the third of the chord are noticeable; parallel fifths and octaves are seldom met with, but what is now called false-relation is common; that is, failure to provide that chromatic alterations from one chord to the next one are not made in the same voice.

APPENDIX N

The Guidonian hand and Solmization

Solmization[k] as applied to psalmody refers to the use of the syllables associated with Guido d'Arezzo (ca. 995-1050) in the recording and reading of music. The mediaeval writers on music made merry with the technicalities involved in Guido's inventions, bequeathing to their successors a highly involved musical theory. As time went on the syllables chosen by Guido took on the syllable *si* at the end.

It is not clear why the English (and the Colonial musicians who followed them) for solmization used only the four syllables *mi-fa-sol-la*. The scale was centered on *mi*, instead of on *ut* or *do*, and became mi-fa-sol-la-fa-sol-la. Traces of this later system may be found in the early nineteenth century or, later still, in the books and singing conventions of the 'fasola' singers.[1] An interesting application of the mi-fa-sol-la method is seen in Lancashire Sol-fa.[m]

It is much more enjoyable to study the early works on musical theory, Simpson, Tans'ur and others, in connection with the exposition of mediaeval theories in Hawkins' *History* (op. cit.) and the articles in Grove. It is possible thereby to acquire an appreciative and informative background necessary to the understanding of much in English and Colonial psalmody otherwise vague.

In studying the illustration of the Guidonian Hand (see page 167) it will be noted that the teacher in Dr. Scholes's *Puritans* is represented

---

[k] See Sir John Hawkins' *A General History of Music*, J. Alfred Novello, London (1853), vol. 1, pp. 153-162, passim. Also Grove, op. cit. articles *Hexachord* and *Solmization*.

[1] See Dr. Jackson's *White Spirituals passim.*

[m] See Dr. Percy A. Scholes's *The Oxford Companion to Music*, Oxford University Press, 1939, article "Lancashire Sol-fa."

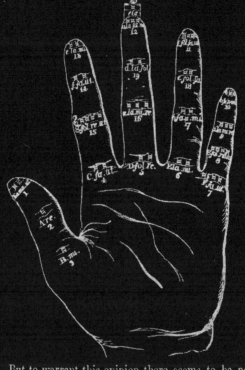

But to warrant this opinion there seems to be no better authority than bare tradition; for in no part of Guido's writings does the mention of the hand occur: nay, it seems from a passage in the manuscript of Waltham Holy Cross, herein before cited, that the hand was an invention posterior in time to that when Guido is supposed to have lived; * its use was to instruct boys in the names and respective situations of the notes of his scale; and for choosing the left hand rather than the right this notable reason is given, 'that it being nearest the heart, the instruction 'derived from thence is likely to make the deeper 'impression on the minds of learners.'

(See p. 123, Appendix N.)

From Sir John Hawkins's *History of Music*, New Edition (1853), London, J. Alfred Novello, vol. 1, p. 161. Another illustration of the Hand, somewhat less informing, is in Grove's *Dictionary*, article "Hexachord." See also Dr. Scholes's *The Puritans and Music*, p. 272.

The names of the lines and spaces may be readily learned by the fingers—as follows:

TREBLE.

BASE.

The lines added to the Staff are called Leger lines, and are only used when the Music extends beyond the compass of the Staff.

See Appendix N.

From *Union Harmony or Music Made Esay*, John Cole, Baltimore, 1828, p. 144. Lowell Mason Library, Library of the School of Music, Yale University.

as using his right hand instead of his left as is shown in Hawkins, Grove, and John Cole. In Hawkins's *History*, Gamma is shown at the end of the thumb, i.e. as *G* now written on the bottom line of the F staff, and the gamut extends upward in Hawkins's *History* to *E*, 20 sounds; or 22 if the two B flats are included, as in the list of sounds listed on page 159 in Hawkins. John Cole's version of the Guidonian Hand shows it in illustrative position, bass and treble, just like a hand. In closely examining the Hawkins illustration it will be noted (with some astonishment) that the sounds are shown skipping about transversely back and forth; it also gives the key to the curious names in Colonial 'grounds.' (viz. d lasol & D solre.)

APPENDIX O

Lowell Mason and the new era

Taking *Mason's Hand-Book of Psalmody*, n.d., London & New York, we get some light on his harmonic skill. He uses the three principal chords of the key, tonic, dominant, and sub-dominant and their first inversions with freedom; he does not use any of the simple chromatic chords in the key, nor does he use secondary seventh-chords with any facility. So far as he goes, however, his harmony is strictly correct according to the ordinary rules. In *The Hallelujah* (1854) he claims a greater variety of chords; the supertonic and mediant chords are frequently heard; less frequent use of I-V and V-I than had been the case; the tonic six-four in the cadence has often given way to the dominant with the third suspended; the preparation and resolution of discords have received more attention. The bass often suffers from lack of variety.

Mason was fond of inverting the tenor and treble, when it could be done with harmonic correctness. See *The Psaltery*, nos. 46, 51b, 123b, 126b, 131b, 135b, 136, 143b, etc.; in these numbers the tenor and treble may change parts; they also illustrate a rhythm in three-four time that is almost an obsession with Lowell Mason, viz. two eighth notes followed by two quarter notes. Considering his self-imposed harmonic limitations Mason had considerable variety in his tunes.

The development of Lowell Mason's talent as a writer of hymn-tunes could be easily studied by an examination of his collections, taken in Chronological order, viz. *Handel & Haydn Society Collection* (1822), *The Choir* (1832), *Boston Academy Collection* (1835), *Modern Psalmist* (1839), *Carmina Sacra* (1840), *Psaltery* (1845), *National Psalmist* (1848), with G. J. Webb; *Cantica Laudis* (1852), with G. J. Webb; *New Cantica Laudis* (?); *Hallelujah* (1854).

Lowell Mason had some unusual ideas regarding music in the large forms by Handel and others. See *The Lyra Sacrs* (1832), preface. He states that (1) the choruses of Handel and Haydn are too difficult for choirs to perform or audiences to comprehend; (2) an orchestra of at least 30-40 and a chorus of 50 are necessary; (3) these choruses are designed for the sole purpose of musical exhibition and display; (4) *The Messiah* was first performed in the theatre and was a theatrical exhibition; (5) there is not the least reason to suppose that Handel ever associated in his own mind, this most sublime of musical compositions, with the humble and spiritual worship of God; (6) devotional feeling is seldom produced in a mixed assembly; (7) that the anthems of the best English composers, with few exceptions, are designed to show the composers' skill in counterpoint, fugue and artificial conceits.

Lowell Mason had a difficult matter to handle in dealing with the tunes of the Billings school, since they were written with very little regard for the rules of harmony. Mason was too well schooled in those rules to print examples of their transgressions, although popular demand for the inclusion of the tunes in the *Handel & Haydn Collection* had to be satisfied. Thereupon he hit on this solution of the matter: in the preface of that collection (edition of 1827, page VI), he printed the following notice:

"The Society is fully aware of the cautious delicacy with which variations should be admitted into tunes that by long use have become familiar and by the power of holy purposes have been in some measure sanctified. They have been careful therefore to retain in general the airs of the several tunes unaltered: but as the longest usage cannot reconcile science and correct taste with false harmony, it has been found indispensably necessary to introduce changes into the accompanying parts. The leading part, however, being unaltered, the change will not be such as to shock even the accustomed ear; while the richness of the harmony cannot fail to increase the delight of every lover of sacred music."

This, however, did not work; for to change the "accompanying parts" is to change the musical atmosphere.

INDEX

Index

174

THE LIBRARY
ST. MARY'S COLLEGE OF MARYLAND
ST. MARY'S CITY, MARYLAND 20686

087362